ALES

FROM AROUND THE WORLD
Stories for Language Learning

JEANNE B. BECIJOS

DOMINIE PRESS, INC.

Publisher: Raymond Yuen
Executive Editor: Carlos Byfield
Project Editor: Liz Parker
Cover Designer: Susan Megling Graphic Design
Text Illustrator: Randol Eagles
Text Designer: Marjorie Taylor

© 1991 Dominie Press, Inc.

Reprinted 1993, 1994, 1998

Published by:

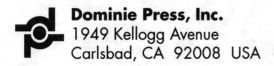

Dominie Press, Inc.
1949 Kellogg Avenue
Carlsbad, CA 92008 USA

ISBN 1-56270-037-5
Printed in U.S.A.
4 5 6 7 8 9 W 01 00 99 98

CONTENTS

ℑNTRODUCTION_____

    Tales from around the World is a collection of folktales from countries representing different areas of the world. The stories are appropriate for ESL, bilingual, and general education students in upper elementary grades, junior high, and high school. The geography, history, and culture of a country is introduced before the student reads the folktale in order to give the reader background information. In this way, ESL instruction fits into a literature-based curriculum. The text was written to provide interesting and motivating reading for intermediate-level ESL students. The material is presented using whole language, including a variety of listening, speaking, reading, and writing activities relating to the selections. Following the Natural Approach, vocabulary and grammatical structures are introduced in written and pictorial context. The stories are presented in an "Into, Through, and Beyond" format to invite the students to become involved in the literature. The Into section delves into the history and culture of the originating country to provide a basis for the tale. The Through section teaches a love for literature through the folktale itself. The Beyond section goes beyond the story, providing insight into morals and values taught by the folktale. Knowledge, comprehension, analysis, synthesis, and evaluation questions (Bloom's Taxonomy) follow each folktale.

    It is possible to sequence the lessons in any order. They have not been sequenced in difficulty and do not rely on the students having studied one unit in order to study the next.

    To facilitate instruction of the material, below you will find information and teaching suggestions to correlate with each section of a tale.

INTO

Knowing the Area

Geography

    The geography questions will be used in conjunction with the world map at the beginning of the book. It would be helpful if there were a classroom map or globe available to use in introducing the textbook and each lesson. As an introduction to the book, you may wish to review the continents and major countries with the class. If possible, guide the students in marking each country as it is encountered in the reading. You may want to make comparisons regarding size and location about new countries with countries previously studied.

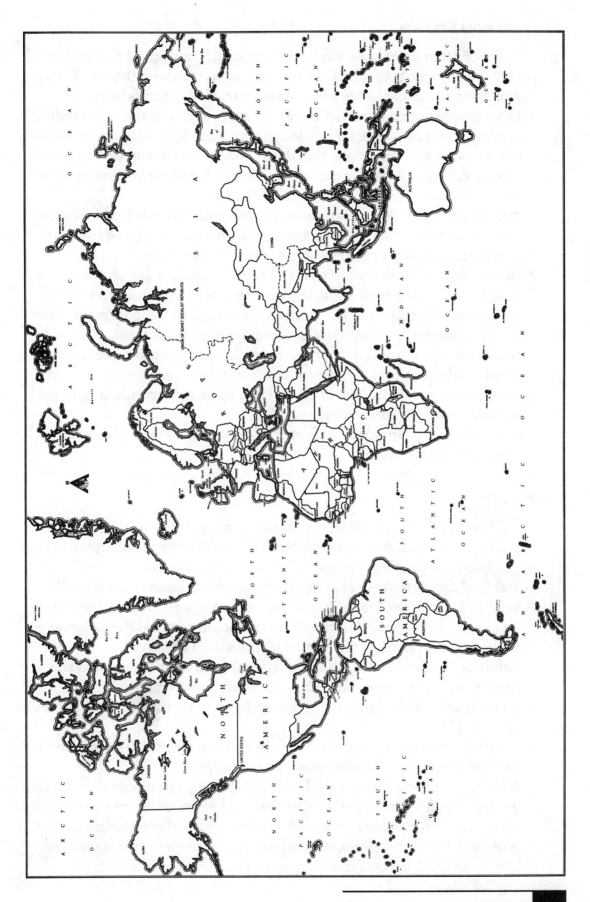

Land and People

This section gives basic information regarding aspects of the land and people of a country. Some students may need assistance with the vocabulary in this section. Following are some ideas for teaching the vocabulary:

- Draw graphic symbols to represent the main words of the information presented, such as a cross for religion, sun and rain for climate, mountains and trees for terrain, a book for education. Write the appropriate word next to the symbol. Students can copy the words and the pictures in their notes.
- Students can brainstorm words associated with the main ideas of the exercise. For example, "land" is associated with forests, plains, lakes, and mountains. Students can copy these words in their notes.
- In one section, students are to use context to place a list of words in a paragraph. To prepare for this section, students may break into groups, each group taking one of the words to be placed in the paragraph. The group discovers the meaning by using a dictionary, the teacher, or another student in the group as reference. Then the group draws a picture that relates to the word and uses the word in a sentence. Each group represents their product to the others in class. The papers can be tacked onto the bulletin board for future reference.
- In some exercises, students can form small groups and help each other with the unknown vocabulary.

History

This section gives basic information regarding the history of a country. Some students may need assistance with the vocabulary and concepts in this part. Here are some ideas for teaching the history exercise:

- You read the section aloud as the students follow along in their books.
- You can draw pictures on the board that explain some of the basic concepts and vocabulary from the section. Then a student can read the paragraphs as the teacher points to the related pictures on the board.
- Before doing the exercise, the students can form small groups and select five unknown words to research and present to the class.
- You may want to do the first question and answer on the board to serve as an example.
- Students can complete the exercise with a partner or a small group to help each other with the difficult words and concepts.
- Making a timeline can be useful in understanding the material. In small groups or individually, the students can make a timeline to correspond with each history section. You may wish to have a giant timeline on the bulletin board to use to combine all the history sections in the textbook. This is an ideal format for making comparisons between countries.

Getting Ready for the Folktale

After the students are familiar with the country of the folktale, there is a section to prepare for the story itself. This section includes discussion questions, journal writing, ideas for brainstorm, cooperative learning strategies, and introduction to vocabulary in order to ready the student for some of the concepts and vocabulary that will be presented in the story. Completing these exercises helps the student focus on the upcoming material. Also, the student has an opportunity to relate previous knowledge to new information.

THROUGH

There are many different ways of presenting the story to the students. You may wish to use one or a combination of the following methods to introduce the story:

- You—or another student—read aloud as the students follow along in their books. You may wish to ask questions intermittently in order to check comprehension.
- Students read the story with a partner, taking turns reading aloud.
- Ask a question about the story or have a student make a prediction about the story. Then assign the students three or more paragraphs to read silently. After reading is finished, answer the question and verify predictions.

Comprehension

Students can answer these questions individually, with partners or in small groups in order to check for overall comprehension of the story.

Deeper Understanding

These questions require higher level thinking skills. You may wish to answer these as a class, individually as a written assignment, or with partners or small groups. Remind the students that often the answers to these questions require extra thought and the answers will not be written word for word in the story.

In all of the stories there is a question about values and traits. These questions are included to model positive character traits and also to reveal important values from the various countries.

Literary Element

Each folktale includes a description, examples, and questions regarding various literary terms. To reinforce these terms, ask questions using these terms with other stories in the book. Students may wish to keep a notebook with definition and examples of the literary terms presented.

BEYOND

The "Beyond" activities solidify the folktale in the students' minds and build additional skills. The vocabulary games help reinforce vocabulary from the stories. Often the students are asked to interview friends and family members in order to relate to the folktale and to give the student practice in oral language. The creative projects included in this section give the students an opportunity to synthesize their learning and practice creativity. When possible, exhibit the projects in the room to help build the students' self-esteem. Each story includes a direction for a writing project in order to give practice in this area. It is recommended to have the students exchange papers and write positive comments and corrections on the partner's paper.

How Coyote Stole Fire

Knowing the Area

"How Coyote Stole Fire" is an American Indian folktale. Below you will find information about the geography, people, and history of the Plains Indians.

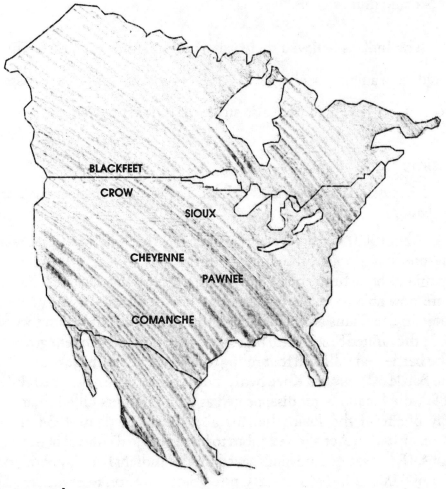

Geography

Look at the map in the front of the book. Answer each question.

   A. Locate the area where the Plains Indians lived. (*Plains* are flat lands without trees.)
   B. In what two countries did the Plains Indians live?

Land and People

Complete each sentence with the correct word.

force	buffalo	mouth
hunters	earth	clothing	language

The Plains Indians were _____. They mainly hunted deer and _____.
             A   B
They used these animals for food, _____, and for making their teepees.
                                C
When the white people moved west, new tribes came to the Plains. To help with communication, the Indians developed a sign _____. They also used
                                                  D
smoke and drum signals.

The Indians believed there was a magical force in nature. This _____
                                                   E
could be in animals or objects. Legends of gods and spirits were passed on by word of _____. There were also stories of the first people on _____.
                  F   G

History

Read the passage about the Plains Indians. Then complete the exercise that follows the passage.

About 30,000 years ago, Indians came to the Americas from Asia. Their lifestyle stayed much the same for thousands of years. In the 1600s, the Spaniards brought the horse and gun to the New World. The Plains Indians were now able to follow buffalo using horses. In the 1800s, white settlers came to the Plains area. They brought disease with them, and whiskey. In 1871 the United States ruled that tribes were not independent governments. The battle that followed that ruling took place in South Dakota in 1890. At the Battle of Wounded Knee two hundred Sioux were massacred (killed). By 1890, the buffalo herds disappeared as white hunters killed them. The old way of life of the Plains Indians also disappeared. In 1934 the Indian Reorganization Act allowed tribes to have political control of their reservations. (Reservations are lands saved for the Indians). Today about one-half of 1,400,000 of Indians in the United States live on reservations.

Match each date on the timeline with the correct letter of the important event.

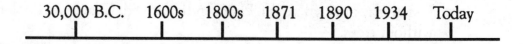

30,000 B.C.   1600s   1800s   1871   1890   1934   Today

A. Indian Reorganization Act passed
B. Battle of Wounded Knee in South Dakota
C. Spaniards brought the horse and gun
D. Whites moved into the Plains area
E. Half of Native Americans live on reservations
F. Ruling that tribes aren't independent governments
G. Indians came from Asia to the Americas

Getting Ready for the Folktale

Journal

What would you like about living the life of a Plains Indian hundreds of years ago?

Vocabulary

Animals were an important part of the Indian way of life.

Write the name of the animal next to the animal's description.

A. no tail
B. stripes on back
C. white tail
D. has claws
E. tail is curled

vulture   squirrel   coyote   chipmunk   frog

Brainstorm

A selfish person cares too much for himself and too little for others. List five things that someone may be selfish about.

THROUGH

Coyote is famous among the Indians for his cleverness and his tricks.

How Coyote Stole Fire

Long ago, there were days when man was very happy. He was new to the world. Spring air blew over the grasses. Man's children grew with the blueberries in the summer sun. In the fall the grains were ready to eat. But winter was not kind to man.

Winter evenings were cold and people became very sad. They were unhappy when winter was near. Parents were afraid for their young children who filled the teepees with laughter. They were fearful for the grandfathers and grandmothers who told the tales of the tribe. Many of the young and old would die during the long winter.

This winter was worse than the winters before. There were many deaths and much crying. Spring came at last. The women sang a sad song for the babies and old ones who had died. Their song of sorrow was carried by the west wind. The wind carried the song over the heads of the buffalos and above the plains. The song travelled to the home of Coyote. The song touched Coyote's heart. He heard it and was saddened.

Coyote went to the village of man. He heard a woman say, "Feel how the sun is warm on our backs. It touches the stones and makes them hot."

Her husband said, "If only we could keep a piece of the sun! It would warm our teepees during the winter."

Coyote felt sorry for the man and woman. He thought of a way to help them. It was always easy for Coyote to think of good ideas. He knew that far away was a mountain. At the very top lived three Fire Beings. These Beings guarded the fire carefully. They were afraid that man would take the fire. Then man would be as strong as the Fire Beings. Coyote didn't like the Fire Beings. He felt that they were selfish. These Beings only cared about themselves.

Coyote climbed to the top of the mountain. The Beings heard Coyote in the bushes. Leaping to their feet, the Beings hunted around the fire. Their eyes were like bloodstones. Their hands were claws, like the claws of a great vulture.

"I hear something! What is it?" cried one of the Beings.

"It is a thief! It wants our fire!" answered another.

The third looked closely and saw Coyote. But she was not afraid. She thought that there was nothing to fear from an ordinary coyote. "It is nothing, sisters. No more than a coyote."

Watching the Beings day and night, Coyote stayed near the

fire. He saw the Beings put wood from the trees into the fire. The wood kept the fire strong. At night, the Beings took turns. Two would sleep as the other guarded. When it was time to change, the Being by the fire got up. She went to the teepee and quickly another would come out to guard.

There was only one time of day or night that the Beings were not careful. In early morning, the cold winds of dawn blew. The Being who was guarding hurried into the teepee. The next sister to watch was always a little slow. She tried to sleep a moment longer in her warm teepee. Coyote saw the slowness and smiled.

Coyote went down the mountain to speak to his friends among the animals. He told them that man feared the cold winter. Of course, man was not like the other animals. He was not lucky enough to have warm fur all over his body. Coyote told the animals about the warm and bright fire. They all agreed to help Coyote bring fire to man.

Coyote ran up to the top of the mountain. Again the Fire Beings cried out, "Thief, thief!" When they saw the coyote, they stopped worrying. Coyote waited quietly. He saw two of the Beings go to sleep in the teepee. All night the Beings took turns. Finally, the cool winds of dawn began to blow.

The Being on guard called, "Sister, hurry! It's dawn, and I'm cold. You come out to watch." The Being quickly entered the teepee.

"Don't worry, I'm coming. Don't shout so loudly." The Being was slow and sleepy. She waited a moment longer in the warm teepee.

Before she came out of the teepee, Coyote grabbed a stick with fire. Holding the wood in his mouth, he ran down the mountain.

Screaming, the Fire Beings ran after him. As fast as the wind, they caught up with Coyote. One of the Beings tried to grab Coyote with her hand. Her fingers touched only the end of the tail. The tail turned white. Today, coyotes' tail are still white. Coyote shouted with pain and dropped the fire. But the other animals were ready to help. Squirrel caught the fire and put it on her back. She moved quickly in the treetops. The fire burned her back, however. Her tail curled up from the pain. Tails of squirrels still curl the same way today.

The Fire Beings went after Squirrel. She threw the fire to Chipmunk. Chipmunk was so scared she couldn't move. As the Beings came near, she turned to run. One of the Beings clawed at Chipmunk. The Being left three stripes on the animal's back. You can still see three stripes on chipmunks' backs today. Chipmunk threw the fire to Frog. The Beings ran after him. One grabbed his tail. Frog jumped high and was free of the Being. He left his tail in the Being's hand, however. That is the reason why frogs have no tails. Frog then threw the fire on Wood. Quickly Wood ate the fire.

The Fire Beings stood around wood. They didn't know how to

get fire out of Wood. They promised it gifts. They sang to it and then they shouted at it. They hit Wood and cut it with their knives. Still Wood would not give them the fire. Finally, the Beings went back to their mountain.

But Coyote knew how to get the fire out of Wood. He went to the village of men. He showed them how to rub two sticks together. The men found fire in the piece of wood. Now man is warm during the cold of winter.

At home again, Coyote felt the force of the west wind. The wind again carried a song to him that touched his heart. This time, it was man's song of joy.

Comprehension

Match two parts to make a correct sentence about the story.

1. Babies and old ones die
2. Coyote decides to help bring
3. Coyote takes the fire
4. The other animals
5. Man learns how to get

A. from the three Beings
B. fire out of Wood.
C. because of the cold winter.
D. help Coyote carry the fire.
E. fire to human beings.

Deeper Understanding

Answer each question, either in a discussion with the class or in your own journal.

1. Name two reasons why you think Coyote helped man.
2. Give an example of how Coyote is clever and has good ideas.
3. According to the story, why don't frogs have tails?
4. Do you think this story about fire and why animals have certain characteristics is true? Why do you think the Indians believed these stories?
5. Name one value that is respected in this folktale, and one trait that is disliked. Choose among the following values:

   selfishness   cruelty

   greed   helpfulness

   patience   humor

6. Do you share the same values as shown in this folktale? Explain.
7. Select one quotation from this folktale that you like. Why did you choose this particular quotation?

Literary Element

Folktale

"How Coyote Stole Fire" is an example of a *folktale*. A folktale is a story told by folks, or the common people. It is usually passed down by word of mouth through generations. Important traditions and beliefs of a people are often taught through folktales.

Read each question. Discuss your answers with the class.

- What time of year do you think the Indians told their folktales most often? Why?
- Picture in your mind the Indians sitting around the fire in their teepees telling folktales. Describe to others what you imagine the Indians doing.

BEYOND

Research

Form small groups. Each group selects a different American Indian tribe. Research and write a report on the different aspects of the tribe, such as food, clothing, location, arts, and religion. Share with others.

Comparison

Make a chart of the major characteristics of each American Indian tribe you researched. Then look for similarities and differences between the tribes.

Writing Project

In "How Coyote Stole Fire," the story explains why the chipmunk has stripes, why the frog has no tail, why the coyote has a white tail, and why the squirrel's tail is curled. Choose an animal that you like. Then write a story about why you think the animal looks the way it does.

Creative Project

Illustrate the story you wrote above.

Ixtla and Popocatepetl_____

Knowing the Area

"Ixtla and Popocatepetl" is an Aztec legend. Below you will find information about the geography, people, and history of this ancient people from Mexico.

Geography

Look at the map at the front of the book. Answer each question.

A. On what continent is Mexico located?
B. What countries border Mexico?

Land and People

Complete each sentence with the correct word.

gods	superb	palaces
silver	civilization	wars

The Aztecs had an elaborate and rich _____. They were expert builders
                A
and constructed large _____ and religious temples. In their religion they
            B
believed in many _____. Human sacrifice (killing of people) was a part of
        C
their religion, also. They usually sacrificed persons caught in _____. The
                    D
Aztecs were also _____ artisans. They made objects and jewelry of gold,
         E
_____, and copper.
 F

History

Read the passage about the Aztec Indians in Mexico. Then complete the exercise that follows the passage.

Hundreds of years ago the Aztecs lived in the Valley of Mexico. Their capital city, Tenochtitlan, was located where Mexico City is today. The government was ruled by an emperor. Montezuma, the last Aztec emperor, ruled from 1502–1520. Hernán Cortés from Spain led his men to the Aztec empire in 1519. Montezuma didn't fight against the Spaniards because he believed Cortés was the white Aztec god Quetzalcoatl.

The Spaniards took over the Aztec empire. They introduced the Spanish language and the Catholic religion to the land. Mexico became an independent country in 1821.

Rewrite each scrambled sentence in the correct word order.

   A. the / Valley / lived / Aztecs / in / Mexico / of / the
   B. emperor / was / the / Montezuma / Aztec / last
   C. Spaniards / fight / Montezuma / didn't / against / the
   D. Catholic / the / introduced / religion / Spaniards / the / to / Mexico
   E. in / Mexico / independent / became / 1821 / country / an

Getting Ready for the Folktale

Journal

In the days of the Aztecs, which would you have preferred to be: the emperor, the empress, a prince, a princess, a servant, an artisan, a warrior, or a peasant? Describe your life.

Group Work

How did Aztec warriors or soldiers fight in the days before guns? Discuss in a group to share with the class. (You may want to use these words: spear, sword, machete, enemy, battle, war.)

Brainstorm

a. As a class, think of famous romantic couples. Choose from literature, from history, from T.V., from songs, and from the movies. Write down their names.

b. Were any of the pairs you chose examples of forbidden love or tragic love? Write forbidden and/or tragic next to these pairs.

c. Discuss these couples' relationships. Talk about what you admire in their relationships. Talk about what you would want to be different in your own relationship.

THROUGH

This Aztec legend tells of forbidden and tragic love.

Ixtla and Popocatepetl

There was once an Aztec emperor in the ancient city of Tenochtitlan. This area is now Mexico City in the great valley of Mexico. The emperor was a strong ruler and kept the enemy tribes beyond the mountains.

The empress had one child, a lovely girl named Ixtla. The emperor and empress prepared her to be the ruler. They gave her much love and attention as she grew.

Ixtla was sweet and kind, and many boys adored her. When she was a young woman, she fell in love. This was a tragic event for her, however. Her father had forbidden her to marry. He trusted none of the young men. After his death, the emperor wanted Ixtla to rule alone.

Ixtla's loved one was a young warrior named Popocatepetl. He was a powerful warrior, yet he was very gentle with Ixtla. Their love was as pure as the white snow on the mountain top. But their love was also as secret as the deepest part of the blue ocean.

The two young people could only spend stolen moments together. Ixtla told the young warrior, "I cannot live without your love. My heart breaks when we are apart."

"Do not fear, my love," Popocatepetl said to Ixtla. "Our love will find a way. I will never leave you. We will be together until the end of time."

Months passed, and the emperor became very ill. Without his strong rule, the enemy tribes attacked the empire. Only the city of Tenochtitlan was still safe. This situation forced the emperor to make a decision. He declared, "The man who defeats the enemy will marry my daughter. This man will also rule over the empire at Ixtla's side."

Ixtla was cold with fear when she heard the decision. What if some other warrior defeated the enemy, and not Popocatepetl? She would prefer to die than to marry another.

The thought of winning the beautiful princess and the empire was wonderful news. The soldiers fought three times as hard as before. Yet the battles were fierce. The enemy surrounded Lake Texacoco near the walls of Tenochtitlan. Many brave men were killed with machetes and spears.

However, one warrior fought more bravely and wisely than all the others. It was Popocatepetl, Ixtla's one true love. He led the other warriors in a defeat of the enemy. The soldiers declared Popocatepetl their leader. The tired but happy warriors rested for the night.

A group of evil soldiers was jealous of Popocatepetl. Without stopping to rest, they ran to the emperor in his palace. They lied and said that Popocatepetl had been killed in battle. The emperor wanted to prepare a proper funeral for the hero. Again lying, the soldiers said Popocatepetl's body had fallen into Lake Texacoco.

The false news came to the ears of the Princess Ixtla. Her father or mother could not comfort her. She cried without stopping. She would not eat or drink. The best healers in the city could not help her. She did not wish to live without Popocatepetl.

Soon she breathed her last breath. At that same moment Popocatepetl came to the gates of the city. The warriors were carrying him on their shoulders. Walking among the cheering people, the group arrived at the emperor's palace. Popocatepetl told the emperor, "We have defeated the enemy! I wish now to marry your fair daughter."

The emperor could not look at the joyful warrior. His heart was filled with sadness. He told the warrior about the false news and Ixtla's death.

The young man's face turned gray in color. He declared he would kill all of the evil soldiers. One by one, he fought the jealous warriors to the death. No one made an effort to stop Popocatepetl.

Next he went to Ixtla's room in the palace. He lifted up the couch with his loved one's body. Carrying the couch in his arms, he walked out of the palace and out of the city. Again, no one tried to stop the warrior.

At some distance from the city, he stopped. His soldiers had followed him. Popocatepetl told the men to build a giant pyramid. Holding the dead princess in his arms, he watched their work. At sunset the job was complete. The red and purple colors of the setting sun reflected on the brilliantly white pyramid. Popocatepetl slowly climbed to the top of the pyramid, carrying the princess. Once at the top, he gently placed the body of his loved one on a golden couch. He slept that night on the pyramid. At dawn he walked down and spoke to the loyal warriors.

"Build another pyramid nearby. It will be a little higher than the first. Then I may look down upon my loved one's grave."

The evening sky was purple when the second pyramid was finished. Popocatepetl climbed his pyramid, carrying a torch lighted by fire. The warriors saw him at last reach the top. The young warrior stood tall and proud. His torch lit up the sky in memory of his loved one. The gray smoke of the torch turned purple and then became red, the color of blood.

As the years passed, the two pyramids became mountains with tops of snow. The mountain to the north of Tenochtitlan is known as Ixtla, the Fair Maiden. The one to the south, a little higher and still smoking, is known as Popocatepetl, the Smoky Mountain. These mountains will be together until the end of time.

Comprehension

Rewrite these events from the story in the correct order.

The emperor is a strong ruler and keeps the enemy away from the empire.
Ixtla falls in love with the strong warrior Popocatepetl.
Popocatepetl builds pyramids for Ixtla and for himself.
Popocatepetl becomes the leader and defeats the enemy.
The emperor promises to give the man who defeats the enemy his daughter's hand and the empire.
Ixtla dies after hearing the false news that Popocatepetl is dead.
The two pyramids turn into mountains.
Jealous soldiers lie to the emperor and tell him Popocatepetl is dead.

Deeper Understanding

Answer each question, either in a discussion with the class or in your own journal.

1. Do you think the emperor made a mistake when he forbade his daughter to marry? Explain.
2. Why do you think the jealous soldiers lied to the emperor?
3. Ixtla died when she heard the false news. Do you think it is possible for someone to will themselves to die? Explain.
4. What statements did Popocatepetl and Ixtla make to each other that came true later? Explain how they came true.
5. Name one value that is respected in this legend, and one trait that is disliked. Give an example of each from the legend. Choose among the following values:

laziness	love
cruelty	wisdom
jealousy	generosity
valor	

6. Give an example of the values shown in this legend that apply to your own life.
7. What scene from this legend will stay in your mind? Describe it to the others.

Literary Element

Simile

A *simile* is a figure of speech that makes a comparison between two different things. It uses the words *like* or *as* to make the comparison.
Examples from the story include:

"Their love was as pure as the white snow on the mountain top."

"But their love was also as secret as the deepest part of the blue ocean." With a simile, a writer can help readers to see things in a fresh, original way. Often, a simile creates an actual picture, or image, in the reader's mind.

- *Write three similes of your own. Compare strength to something in nature, to a manmade object, and to a feeling. Use this form:*

   Strength is as _____ as _____ .

BEYOND

Research

Research the story of "Romeo and Juliet." Describe the similarities and differences between this story and the Aztec legend.

Survey

Ask your family about some rules they have established that are for your own good. For example, setting a time that you must be home at night, not allowing you to miss school, etc. Then ask them if they would forbid you to marry someone you loved. If so, find out in what situation.

Creative Project

Look up different Aztec art forms and art objects. In groups or individually, draw these art works and display them.

Writing Project

Imagine that you are Popocatepetl or Ixtla. You are very lonely and miss your loved one during the war. Write him/her a letter.

The Seven Young Sky Women ____

Knowing the Area

"The Seven Young Sky Women" is a folktale from the islands of the Philippines. Below you will find information about the geography, people, and history of the Philippines.

Geography

Look at the map in the front of the book. Answer each question.

    A. What continent is to the west of the Philippines?
    B. Name three countries that are near the Philippines.

Land and People

Complete each sentence with the correct word.

schools	**English**	**president**
islands	**corn**	**important**

      The Philippines is a group of more than 7000 islands. People live on only about 880 of the _____ . More than half of the people work the land. They
           A
farm mostly rice, coconut, _____ , and sugar. The official national languages
                    B
are Pilipino (based on Tagalog) and _____ . Education is _____ in this
                            C   D
country. There are many _____ of higher education. More than half of the
                  E
people are of the Roman Catholic religion. The country is now a democracy
with a _____ .
      F

History

Read the passage about the Philippines. Then complete the exercise that follows the passage.

People have lived in the Philippines for more than 250,000 years. In 1542, the Spanish explorer Villalobos gave the Philippines its name in honor of King Philip II of Spain. The islands were a colony of Spain for over 300 years. The Spanish influence is seen today in the country's Roman alphabet, the architecture of the churches, and the Christian religion. After the Spanish-American War in 1898, Spain gave the Philippines to the United States. The United States began to prepare the country for independent government.

During World War II, Japan occupied the islands. After the war ended in 1946, the country became an independent republic. Today it is governed by a president.

Rewrite each scrambled sentence in the correct word order.

    A. 250,000 years / people / for over / have lived / in the Philippines
    B. 300 years / a colony / the islands / were / of Spain / for
    C. gave / the Philippines / to the U.S. / Spain / in 1898
    D. the islands / during / Japan / occupied / World War II
    E. independent / today / the Philippines / is / republic / an

Getting Ready for the Folktale

Journal

In the story "The Seven Young Sky Women," the young women can fly. Write about what it would be like to fly like a bird. Where would you go?

Vocabulary

*Look at the first picture in the story. Point out the **turban** that the man is wearing on his head. Also point to the **pond** of water. Find the second picture in the story. Point to the **bag** that is hanging in the **rafters**.*

Debate

In the story, Itung tells a lie. Form two groups. One group supports the idea that it is okay to lie in some situations. The other group is against lying in all cases. The two groups first meet alone to discuss their ideas. Then the groups debate the question.

THROUGH

This Filipino folktale is a story of love lost.

The Seven Young Sky Women

Long ago there was a young man named Itung. One day he decided to take a journey to visit his aunt. After a few hours of travel, he came to her home. "Good day, Aunt," said Itung.

"Oh," replied the woman, "it's good you came by today. I made a new discovery. There is a pond a distance from here. Every day at noon seven lovely young women go there to bathe."

"Very good," said the young man. "Maybe I'll want to marry one of these young women."

"Fine, fine," smiled the aunt. "Now, take a dozen bananas with you. The women are guarded by pet monkeys. You can throw bananas to the monkeys to keep them busy."

So the young man took the bananas and left. When he arrived at the pond he hid himself. After a while he heard a noise in the air. Looking up, he saw seven women flying in the sky. They landed near the pond. Itung could not tell the maidens apart. They were all identical in their beauty.

The women removed their clothes to bathe. Seven monkeys watched over the clothes. Itung threw the bananas to the side, and six of the monkeys ran to eat them. Only one monkey remained, watching over the clothes of the youngest maiden. Itung threw banana after banana, but the monkey would not move. The young man then threw the last banana, the largest of all, and the monkey ran off to eat it. Itung jumped up, grabbed the clothes of the young woman, and ran to his aunt's house.

"Good work, Itung," the aunt said in praise. "Give me the dress and return to the pond. Hide yourself again in the bushes."

Itung did as he was told. Once hidden, he saw the maidens get ready to leave. One by one the women got out and dressed. At last the youngest came out. She began to look frantically for her clothes.

"Sisters, a terrible thing has happened! My clothes have disappeared." The maiden began to cry. The other sisters helped her look for her clothes.

At last the oldest one said, "Youngest sister, I am sorry but we must leave. It is late and we have to return to Father. Come home when you find your dress. We'll be looking for you, Inay."

In great distress, the young woman watched her sisters fly away. She lay down on the ground and began to weep loudly.

"Why are you crying? What can I do to help you?" asked Itung as he came out of his hiding place.

"Oh," cried Inay. "Who are you? Don't come near me!"

The young man took off his turban and threw it to Inay. "Wrap yourself in that." The maiden dressed herself but continued crying. Itung took the young woman in his arms, saying, "Please stop crying."

Inay pushed him away. "Are you the one who took my dress? If so, give it back to me! I can't return home to my sisters and father without my clothes."

"Oh, no, it wasn't I," lied Itung. "But as it is impossible for you to return home, I want you to stay with me. Please be my wife. We will then never be separated as long as we both live."

Inay thought sadly about her situation. She did not want to agree, but had no choice. "Very well," said the maiden, "I am forced to accept your offer. But understand that if I find my dress someday, I will return home. Even if we have children, I will still fly back to my family."

"Don't be sad. I know we'll be happy together. One day you will love me as I love you," said Itung tenderly. Inay said nothing, but her crying increased. The young man picked her up and carried her across his shoulders.

Itung showed the maiden to his aunt. She was very happy to hear about the wedding plans. Then Itung carried the woman to his own village. All the people stopped in wonder. The chief, Itung's father, looked out of his house and saw his son. "Itung, where did you find this lovely woman? Come, let me see her." All of the family came to meet the young maiden.

On the day of the wedding the aunt came. She went to Itung's house and spoke to him. "Itung, tie this bag of mine up high in the rafters of the roof. It is not to be opened," she said. The young man did as told.

After a year, Inay gave birth to a baby girl. The girl had the looks of her mother. She was like a leaf taken from the same betel-nut tree. One day when she was older the girl noticed the bag in the rafters. "Mother, I want that bag up there."

Her mother continued with her sewing. "No, it belongs to Aunt. She will be angry if we get it."

Itung heard the girl's request. He said angrily, "Listen to your mother."

The child began to cry. She jumped onto her mother's lap.

"Daughter, look what you have done with your jumping! I have pricked my finger with the needle." There was blood from her finger on the sewing.

The daughter cried for the bag all day and night. She cried until she had no more voice. Finally, Itung agreed to take down the bag. The girl opened it. Inside was the mother's dress.

"It is my dress!" cried out Inay. "I must go home to my kingdom at once. This child is from your land and I can't bring her with me. Take good care of her, my husband."

Itung was so upset he could not speak.

"Husband, do you feel bad because you lied to me? If you like, you can visit me. I live in the place where the moon rises and the sun sets." The young woman dressed herself, kissed the child, and rose up into the air.

Itung picked up his daughter and took her to his parents. "Father, Mother, please watch my daughter. I must search for Inay. I can't live without her."

The young man walked through long grass and short, not caring if it was night or day. At times he would fall over and sleep, completely exhausted. Then once awake he would continue. His body became covered with cuts from the bushes.

After a long time, Itung met an old man. "Help me, please. I'm looking for my wife. She lives where the moon rises and the sun sets."

"Let's ask the birds," said the old man. The man whistled, and all of the birds came. None of the birds knew of the place, however. Then the old man went to the seashore and whistled again. An eel came out of the water. The eel knew the answer. "You must pass through that mountain toward the west," said the eel. "Then go downhill seven times and uphill seven times until you come to the place."

Itung thanked the man and the eel, then travelled until he reached the home of Inay. He saw the large house of a chief. He asked and received permission to go up the house ladder. Inside, he told the chief he wanted to take his wife home with him.

"Are you Itung?" asked the chief. "You can take her back home on one condition. You must recognize her among her sisters."

Seven young women were brought out of their rooms. Itung looked at each, but there was indeed no difference. "May I look at their fingers?" Itung asked the chief.

"Why not?" answered the chief. "Try your best. But if you don't know her on your first guess, you can't have her."

The young man looked at all the hands of the maidens. "This one, Chief, is my wife. I recognize the mark of a needle on her smallest finger."

"You can take her," said the chief, "for she is indeed your wife."

Inay smiled at her husband. "I am glad you knew me, Itung. I missed my daughter very much. And I forgive you for lying to me. I know now that I love you as much as you love me." And the two returned home to their daughter.

Comprehension

Match two parts to make a correct sentence about the story.

Effects		Causes	
1.	Itung hid the maiden's dress	A.	because he saw the mark on her finger.
2.	Inay can't return to her home	B.	because she found her dress.
3.	The little girl was crying	C.	because he wanted to marry her.
4.	Inay pricked her finger	D.	because he couldn't live without her.
5.	Inay went to her father's home	E.	because the little girl jumped on her.
6.	Itung searched for his wife	F.	because she wanted the bag.
7.	Itung chose the correct sister	G.	because Itung hid her dress.

Deeper Understanding

Answer each question, either in a discussion with the class or in your own journal.

1. Itung hid Inay's dress. Do you think he should have lied to her? Explain.
2. The aunt helped Itung and Inay get married. Then what did she do that led to their separation?
3. Perhaps it was a good idea for Inay to return to her father's home. Explain why.
4. What is the expression used that means the little girl looks like her mother?
5. How do we know that Itung really loved his wife?
6. Name three magical elements of the story.
7. Choose one value from the choices that is respected in this story, and one trait that is disliked. Give an example of each from the story.

   love   disloyalty

   greed   dishonesty

   motherhood   freedom

Literary Element

Sequence

The *sequence* of events in a story refers to the time order of events. It is important to understand which event comes first and how it leads to the next event.

Below are events from the story. Rewrite them in the correct sequence.

Inay returns to her home after finding her dress.
Itung asks an old man for directions to Inay's home.
Itung takes Inay home and marries her.
Itung's aunt tells him about the seven maidens near the pond.
The eel tells Itung where to find Inay's home.
Inay is crying because she can't return home with her sisters.
Inay and Itung return home to their daughter.
Inay and Itung have a daughter who looks like her mother.

BEYOND

Game

Divide into two teams. Each team writes eight questions about the story to ask the other team. Then a representative from one team goes in front of the class. The other team asks him/her one question. Alternate teams to answer questions. The team who answers the most questions correctly wins.

Research

In the story, Itung climbed up a house ladder to the home of Inay's father. Find out about these kind of houses in the Philippines. What are they made of? Why are house ladders needed? Why are the houses raised high above the ground?

Creative Project

Make a map of Itung's island. Draw and name places from the story, such as the aunt's home, the pond, Itung's village, the eel at the seashore, and Inay's home. Include a marker indicating north, south, east, and west.

Writing Project

Itung was very unhappy when he couldn't find Inay. Make a poster offering a reward for Itung. The poster will include who is lost, a description of the person, where the person was last seen, and a reward for finding the missing person. Work with a partner or in groups.

The Gentle Folk

Knowing the Area

"The Gentle Folk" is a folktale from Argentina. Below you will find information about the geography, people, and history of Argentina.

Geography

Look at the map in the front of the book. Answer each question.

A. On what continent is Argentina located?
B. What country is west of Argentina?
C. What other countries border Argentina?

Land and People

Complete each sentence with the correct word.

climate	mountains	write	Italy
hot	country	penguins	Spanish

Argentina is the second largest _____ in Latin America. It is also a land
                   A
of great contrasts. In the far south, the land is very cold. Many _____ live
                                             B
there. In the north it is _____ and humid. Animals such as jaguars and pumas
                    C
live there. To the west are the high Andes _____ covered with snow. Most
                                         D
of the people live in the pampas. This land is flat, grassy, and has a mild

_____.
 E

The national language of Argentina is _____. About ninety percent of
                                         F
the people are Roman Catholic. Education is taken seriously in this country.
A very high percentage of Argentinians can read and _____. Nearly ninety
                                       G
percent of the people are of European descent, most from Spain or _____.
                                                  H
There are very few native Indians.

History

Read the passage about Argentina. Then complete the exercise that follows the passage.

Spanish settlers first came to Argentina in the 1500s. The native Indians resisted the Spaniards. Many of the Indians were killed. Argentina became a colony of Spain. The country became independent of Spain in 1816. General José de San Martín led the fight against the Spanish. The 1800s were a time of economic progress. Many people from Europe immigrated to Argentina.

For about one hundred years, Argentina has been ruled mostly by military dictators. The dictator Juan Peron ruled from 1946 to 1955, and then again from 1973 to 1974. Today Argentina still has economic and political problems.

Rewrite each scrambled sentence in correct word order.

A. to Argentina / first came / Spanish / in the 1500s / settlers
B. were killed / many of / by / the Indians / the Spanish
C. San Martín / the fight / led / from Spain / for independence
D. many people / in the 1800s / to Argentina / from Europe / immigrated
E. twelve years / the dictator / ruled / Juan Peron / Argentina / for

Getting Ready for the Folktale

Discussion

"The Gentle Folk" is a story about an animal called the guanaco. Look at its picture in the story. Describe it. It has a more famous relative. Do you know the name of its relative?

Cluster

The story is about gentle people. Write the word gentle on a piece of paper and circle it. Think of words that relate to gentle. You can use synonyms, people, actions, things, and so on. Be imaginative! Write these descriptions around the circle and connect them to the circle with lines.

Journal

The Gentle Folk live in a perfect world. Describe what a perfect world would be like for you.

Group Work

In the story, the leader of the Gentle Folk gives his people gold, silver, and jewels. Make a list of the names and colors of eight different jewels.

This Argentine story tells of the origin of the unique animal called the guanaco.

THE GENTLE FOLK

A guanaco is an animal that looks like a small camel without a hump. It is tall, proud looking, and yellow and white in color. At times the leader of a group of these animals will stand on top of a hill. It appears to be watching out for the others. When a guanaco knows that death is near, the animal heads south. In the Valley of Gallegos in Patagonia, the guanacos go to die. Here is a story about how these animals came to exist.

Long ago, before there were horses on the land, there lived a gentle people. These folks knew nothing of anger, pain, or sickness. Animals and birds did not fear them. The women were more graceful and the men were much kinder than any on earth today. The wind was never too cold and the sun was never too hot. The birds were brighter in color and flowers smelled sweeter than those of present days.

The leader of these people was called the Golden Prince. He was loved by all for his goodness and his wisdom. At times the prince of the Gentle Folk held great celebrations. During the festivities, he gave the people gold and silver and diamonds and jewels. The people enjoyed looking at them for their beauty alone. The animals and birds came to join in the fun. The air was filled with joyful song and the scent of flowers.

There was only one thing the Gentle Folk could not do. The prince told them never to go to the great dark forest that was north of their land. On the other side of the forest lived some terrible men who did evil.

Capa was a young, strong member of the Gentle Folk. He loved beautiful and colorful birds. One day he saw a bird that was green and blue and gold, with a long white tail. Capa tried to touch the bird, but the bird flew away. The young man didn't realize that the bird was afraid of man. All of the birds Capa knew were at peace with the Gentle Folk. The more the bird flew away, the more Capa wanted to hold the bird. Capa followed the bird into a dark forest. It was so dark that he couldn't see the sun or stars from inside the forest.

On the other side of the forest Capa saw some strange people. They ate animals and wore animals' skins for clothes. When they saw Capa, the men jumped at him. They tore off his clothes of gold thread and his ruby ring.

Then the people fought to get the beautiful things. They completely destroyed the clothes of gold. Terrified, Capa turned and ran back to his own people.

Capa told his story to the prince. Hearing it, the prince was sad at heart. "You have now seen greed and selfishness," said the prince.

"It is very bad for all of us. These strange people will not rest until they find our riches."

The prince called all his people together. Then Capa sang of the evil of the people on the other side of the forest. The Gentle Folk were saddened by the tale.

"We have two choices," said the Golden Prince. "We can stay and fight the men. I can give you weapons and show you how to kill. But if you learn to fight and bring death, you will change. You will never be a gentle people again. You will even fight your own people. You will turn against the animals and they will turn against you. The days of the bright and beautiful colors will be finished. I know you like to play with beautiful jewels and gold." The prince held up a handful of jewels and gold. They shone brightly in the sun. "If you learn to fight, you will learn greed. Then you will hide your jewels so no one can steal them."

The people were fearful of what could happen. "What is the other choice, kind Prince?" they asked.

"Our other choice is to change ourselves into a new form. Then we can escape unnoticed. We can join our friends, the birds and the animals."

Every single one of the the Gentle Folk agreed to change themselves into a new form. No one wanted to become like the strange people.

At that moment, the Gentle Folk heard their enemy coming. The prince quickly led his people away. All of their animal friends escaped with them. Once they arrived at a great valley, the prince stopped the group. "I will now change us into a new form for a while. We will become animals. But we will not bite or give out poison or hurt living things." With a wave of his hand, the prince changed the people into guanacos. All the men, women, and children became proud and graceful animals. Their color was yellow and white, like the gold and silver of their clothes. Once his friends had changed, the prince turned himself into the leader of the guanacos.

Even to this day, the guanaco leader will stand on a rock and guard his group. And, just like the first guanacos, the animals go to a valley to die. In the spot where a guanaco dies, a flower appears. The flower is as blue as the sky and has tips of gold. When the last guanaco dies, the evil men will be gone. At that time the flowers will change back into people. Once again, the Gentle Folk will have their land. Kindness and joy and beauty and gentleness will be theirs once more.

Comprehension

Match two parts to make a correct sentence about the story.

	Effects		**Causes**
1.	The Gentle Folk loved their prince	A.	because it guards the group of guanacos.
2.	The Gentle Folk weren't to go past the dark forest	B.	because they wanted his clothes and ruby.
3.	The bird flew away from Capa	C.	because he was good and wise.
4.	Capa followed the bird	D.	because it was afraid.
5.	The strange men jumped at Capa	E.	because the evil people will be gone.
6.	The Gentle Folk changed form	F.	because terrible men lived there.
7.	The guanaco leader stands on a rock	G.	because they wanted to escape from the evil people.
8.	Someday the Gentle Folk will return	H.	because he wanted to touch it.

Deeper Understanding

Answer each question, either in a discussion with the class or in your own journal.

1. Why do you think the people are called the Gentle Folk?
2. What place does the land of the Gentle Folk remind you of?
3. Are people today more like the Gentle Folk or the strange men? Explain your answer.
4. Name one value that is respected in this legend, and one value that is disliked. Give an example of each from the story. Choose among the following values:

gentleness	greed
anger	respect
cooperation	dishonesty

Literary Element

Conflict

Conflict in a story is the struggle between opposing forces. Almost all stories have one or more points of conflict. A conflict can be (1) a person against society; (2) a person against nature; (3) a person against another person; or (4) a person struggling with himself/herself.

- *Look at the four types of conflict. Which type of conflict is found in this story? Explain.*

- Finish these two sentences regarding the winner of the conflict in this story.

    A. In one way, the strange men were the winners because _____ .

    B. In another way, the Gentle Folk were the winners because _____ .

BEYOND

Game

Play a vocabulary game with names of animals. Divide into pairs or small groups. See how many names of animals each group can list within fifteen minutes. You may use a dictionary for spelling. Work together, passing the paper around the group so that each person has a chance.

Research

Research the animal called the guanaco. (If you have problems finding information on this animal, you can research the llama, its relative.) Write the information you find into a report. Include these facts about the animal: its home, food, means of reproduction, movement, skin cover, and a special feature of the animal.

Creative Project

With a partner or in small groups, make a word collage about the story. Look in newspapers or magazines. Find words or phrases that relate to the story. Cut out and paste these words on poster board to make a collage.

Writing Project

Write a poem about the guanaco or another animal of your choice. If possible, find a picture of the animal to help you in your description. First, describe the animal in clear detail, including its appearance, special abilities, and personality. Then put your description into poetic form. It isn't necessary to rhyme. For example:

THE BIRD
A large, regal bird sits on a branch
At the very top of a tall, tall tree.
Its wings are spread out far and wide.
Is the bird coming or going?

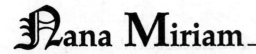ana Miriam

INTO

Knowing the Area

"Nana Miriam" is a legend from Niger. Below you will find information about the geography, people, and history of Niger.

Geography

Look at the map in the front of the book. Answer each question.

    A. On what continent is Niger located?
    B. Name three countries that border on Niger.
    C. What country south of Niger has a similar name?

Land and People

Complete each sentence with the correct word.

    difficult   **Desert**   **Songhai**

    River   **language**   **rice**

Niger is the largest country in West Africa. It is named after the Niger

_____, Africa's third-longest river. The north area of Niger is part of the
  A

Sahara _____. The best land for growing crops is near the Niger River. Crops
     B

grown include peanuts, _____, and millet.
           C

Niger does not have a big population. People are spread out, and it is

_____ to bring schools and teachers to everyone. The different groups of
 D

people in Niger include the Hausa, the _____, and the Fulani tribes. The
                     E

official _____ is French. Some of the people are nomads. This means they
     F

move often from one place to another.

History

Read the passage about Niger. Then complete the exercise that follows the passage.

The Republic of Niger was the scene of several of West Africa's former empires. One of these was the Songhai Empire, lasting from the 8th to the 16th century. The people were farmers and traders. They were very prosperous and cultured. Their kings developed a large commercial empire. People from the Songhai group still live in Niger. The country became a territory of French West Africa in 1904. Niger gained independence in 1960. Niger had great difficulties during the drought of the late 1960s and early 1970s. (A drought is a long period of little or no rain.) Due to the problems of lack of food, there was unrest in the country. The military took over in 1974.

Rewrite each scrambled sentence in the correct word order.

   A. lasted from / the / 8th / century / 16th / the Songhai Empire / to
   B. Songhai / the / were / farmers / and traders / prosperous
   C. Niger / there / Songhai people / still / living / are / in
   D. became / 1904 / territory / West Africa / of / Niger / a / in / French
   E. in / became / Niger / independent / 1960
   F. suffered / Niger / during / period / of drought / a / '60s and '70s/ in the

Getting Ready for the Folktale

Discussion

In the legend "Nana Miriam," the girl is very brave. Do you think girls can be as brave as boys? Discuss your answer and give reasons.

Research

In this legend from Africa, the people suffer from a famine. A famine is a time of extreme lack of food and much hunger. Ask others and read about the problems of famine in Africa during modern times.

Vocabulary

*Look at the pictures from the story. Point to the **hammer** in the girl's hand and the **pouch** hanging on a **string** around the girl's **neck**.*

Group Work

Why are crops, the tribe, a village, a lance, and a hammer important to African farmers? In small groups, discuss and write the answer to this question.

This legend from Niger tells of a brave and powerful young woman.

ℌana Miriam

Long ago a man and his daughter lived near the great River Niger. They were members of the Songhai tribe. Fara Maka was taller and stronger than any man of his tribe. His daughter Nana Miriam was also tall and strong. In addition, she was very beautiful. All of the Songhai young men wanted to marry her.

Fara Maka taught his daughter many wonderful things. He taught her about animals and fish. She learned their ways and their secrets. On a warm evening, she would sit on the bank of the River Niger. There she silently watched the beauty of nature. She listened to the music of the night. And she saw the moon throw its face on the river.

Nana Miriam knew well of the magic of nature. But her father taught her other magic as well. He gave her a magic powder and showed her its powers. He explained that she also had powers from within. "My daughter," said Fara Maka, "you have great magic inside you. You can get whatever you want, if you think very hard. But remember, your power must always be used for good. You will have a happy life if you use your magic wisely." Nana Miriam listened to everything her father told her. She put the magic powder in a special pouch and hung it around her neck.

Then terrible times came to the villages. A monster appeared near the River Niger. This monster took the form of a hippopotamus. He ate without ever stopping. At night he broke into the rice fields and ate all the crops. A time of famine came to the people. Many people died of hunger. Hunters from everywhere tried to kill the hippopotamus. As the creature could change shape, no one was able to destroy the monster.

"Daughter," said Fara Maka, "I must try to kill this creature. Stay and watch our farm." Fara Maka took all of his lances with him. When he saw the terrible creature near the river, he jumped back in fear. There was a ring of fire around the animal's neck. Fara Maka threw lance after lance, but the flames ate every one. The hippopotamus laughed at the man's useless efforts. Then the creature turned away and went back to sit on the river bank.

Fara Maka returned, very angry at his defeat. He told his daughter, "Nana Miriam, I have failed. I cannot destroy the monster. People speak of a great hunter of the Tomma tribe. Maybe he will help us."

The mighty hunter Kara-Digi-Mao-Fosi-Fasi was happy to help the Songhai people. He was confident he could defeat the hippopotamus. With him he brought his one hundred and twenty dogs. To honor the hunter and his dogs, Fara Maka prepared a great feast. Each dog had a bowl of rice and meat, and the hunter had all the food he wanted. In a short time not one bit of this food remained.

After eating, the hunter and dogs went to find the monster. Quickly the dogs picked up the smell of the creature. Kara-Digi-Mao-Fosi-Fasi set loose his dogs. One dog after another attacked the hippopotamus. But one by one the monster ate the dogs. In terror, Kara-Digi-Mao-Fosi-Fasi ran home to his village.

Fara Maka was unhappy to hear about the defeat of the great hunter. He sat in the shadow of a large tree and put his head in his hands.

"Father, I want to fight the monster," said Nana Miriam.

"Many strong and powerful men have tried and failed. Do you really think you can kill the creature?" asked Fara Maka.

"I must try. The people in the villages are dying," said Nana Miriam.

"Then go, my brave daughter. Use your powers well," responded Fara Maka.

Nana Miriam walked down to the River Niger. She saw the hippopotamus eating a field of rice.

"Good morning," said Nana Miriam.

"This is a good joke," answered the hippopotamus. "Here comes a girl to defeat me. You father lost his lances. The great hunter Kara-Digi-Mao-Fosi-Fasi lost all his dogs. Do you really think you can destroy me?" The monster started laughing until tears came to his eyes.

"We will soon find out. Prepare to fight. Only one of us will be alive to tell this tale." Nana Miriam stood bravely before the monster.

In answer, the hippopotamus breathed huge flames of fire. He made a ring of fire around himself.

Nana Miriam reached into the pouch around her neck. She took out a handful of magic powder and threw it at the fire. Instantly the fire turned into water.

"Do you think you can defeat me with magic? My magic is far stronger than yours!" Suddenly a huge wall of iron came up around the hippopotamus. Nana Miriam used the power of her mind. In an instant a magic hammer appeared in her hand. With her great strength, she destroyed the iron wall with one strike of the hammer.

The hippopotamus began to feel afraid. He changed himself into a small river running into the Niger.

Again Nana Miriam threw her magic powder. The river disappeared and there was the hippopotamus shaking before her.

"Daughter! How are you doing?" It was Fara Maka. He had

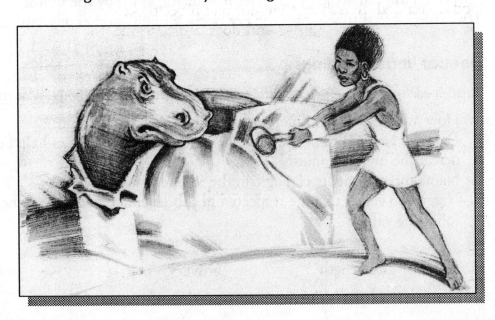

come to see what was happening. The monster turned and started to run right at the man. Just as her father was about to be killed, Nana Miriam grabbed the hippopotamus. She picked him up by his back foot and swung him across the Niger. The monster hit the river bank with a loud noise and died instantly.

Fara Maka cried out, "What a great daughter I have!" He took her to the nearest village. Proudly, he told everyone about his daughter's actions. The village musician wrote a song about Nana Miriam and the Hippopotamus. Soon all the villages in the Songhai tribe were singing of her adventure. And no longer did the people die of hunger.

Comprehension

Tell whether each sentence is true or false.

1. Fara Maka and his daughter were from the Tomma tribe.
2. Nana Miriam was tall, strong, and beautiful.
3. Nana Miriam's father taught her about people and magic.
4. A monster hippopotamus ate the people's crops.
5. Fara Maka defeated the monster with his lances.
6. A great hunter lost his ten dogs to the hippopotamus.
7. Fara Maka's daughter was afraid of the monster.
8. Nana Miriam used her magic and strength to defeat the hippopotamus.
9. Nana Miriam saved her brother from being killed by the monster.
10. The Songhai tribe sang a song of Nana Miriam and her adventures.

Deeper Understanding

Answer each question, either in a discussion with the class or in your own journal.

1. How was the monster different from a regular hippopotamus?
2. Describe Nana Miriam's personality. How did these qualities help her defeat the hippopotamus?
3. Name three elements of magic in the legend.
4. Name two values that are respected in this legend. Choose from the following values:

peace	generosity
strength	bravery
friendship	gentleness

Literary Element

Plot

The sequence of events in a story is called the *plot*. In most stories, one event follows the next. The plot is what happens in a story.

- *Select the five most important events from the plot of the legend "Nana Miriam." Write them in the order they occurred.*

BEYOND

Game

Play a game of "Win, Lose, or Draw" with vocabulary from the story. Divide into two groups. One group writes a word from the story on a small piece of paper. Then a member of the opposite group goes to the chalkboard and illustrates that word for his/her team. Have someone record how long it took to guess the word. Repeat each step with the other group. The team that guesses their word in the shorter amount of time scores a point.

Survey

Make a survey of friends and family. Ask them this question: "Give an example of a brave action of a girl or woman. The example can be from personal experience, from the news, or from history." Combine the results into a chart, indicating which women were named most frequently.

Creative Project

Divide into groups of five. Look at the five major events you wrote in answer to the question from the section entitled Literary Element. Each person from the group makes a cartoon drawing of one event. Tape the five drawings together to make a cartoon strip of the legend.

Writing Project

Write a newspaper article about the adventures of Nana Miriam. Use the style of a newspaper reporter. Write a headline for your story. Remember to include the answers to who, what, when, and where in the first paragraph.

The Demon of Stone Mountain

Knowing the Area

"The Demon of Stone Mountain" is a Vietnamese folktale. Below you will find information about the geography, people, and history of Vietnam.

Geography

Look at the map at the front of the book. Answer each question.

   A. Name three countries and the ocean that are near Vietnam.
   B. What continent is Vietnam on?

Land and People

Complete each sentence with the correct word.

religion	**farming**	**important**
climate	**rice**	**literature**

Vietnam has a tropical _____. There are often heavy rains during the
                      A
year. The economy of Vietnam depends on agriculture (the _____ of the
                                                          B
land). The main farm product is _____. Fishing is also _____ to the economy.
                                 C   D
Most of those who practice a _____ are Buddhists. Many of them also
                              E
worship the spirits of animals and plants. The family is a valued element of
the Vietnamese. Poetry has been the most popular form of _____ in Vietnam.
                                                           F

History

Read the passage about Vietnam. Then complete the exercise that follows the passage.

The Vietnamese people set up a state independent from China in 939. Nguyen Anh named the area Vietnam in 1802. He declared himself its emperor. France took control of Vietnam from 1858 to 1883. The French wanted the land as a colonial power. In 1954, the Vietnimh defeated the French and Vietnam was divided into two nations—North and South Vietnam.

The Viet Cong rebelled against South Vietnam in 1957. The fighting then developed into the Vietnam War. The United States became involved in the war in the 1950s. Many American soldiers were killed in the Vietnam War. The United States ended its participation in the war in 1973. The war was very destructive. Much of the country was in ruins. In 1976, the Communists unified North and South Vietnam into one country. About a million people left Vietnam as the war ended. Many Vietnamese came to the United States as refugees.

Match each date on the timeline with the letter of the important event listed below.

| 939 | 1802 | 1858–1883 | 1957 | 1973 | 1976 |

A. The Communists unified North and South Vietnam into one country.
B. The Vietnamese set up a state independent from China.
C. The United States ended their participation in the Vietnam War.
D. Nguyen Anh united the country and called it Vietnam.
E. France took control of Vietnam.
F. The Viet Cong rebelled against the government of south Vietnam.

Getting Ready for the Folktale

Journal

What are the similarities and differences between your culture and the Vietnamese culture?

Group Work

One partner looks up the definition of oxen, and the other looks up the definition of wink. One partner gives the other partner directions on drawing a picture that describes the word. Remember, don't tell the person the word. Try to let the partner guess the meaning from the drawing.

Vocabulary

In the story a farmer uses a plow to help him prepare the ground. Look at the pictures in the folktale and point to a picture of a farmer using a plow to prepare his field. In the same picture point to the laughing mountain and to the gold inside.

Brainstorm

A greedy person is a person who selfishly wants more. For example, he or she may want more possessions, more money, or more power. In whole or small groups, brainstorm names of people in history and in the news who are greedy, and what they want. (Examples: Hitler was greedy for power. A drug dealer is greedy for money.)

THROUGH

This is a Vietnamese folktale that tells about the results of greed.

The Demon of Stone Mountain

In the land of Vietnam there lived two brothers. Their mother and father had just died from illness. The younger brother went to the funeral to bury his parents. The older brother, however, stayed at home to divide the possessions of the parents. As he was very greedy, he wanted the fortune for himself. He hid all his parents' money and precious possessions.

When the younger brother came home, he looked around in surprise.

"Tell me, honored brother," said Tran, the younger brother. "Where is the fortune of our parents? There is nothing here."

"Oh, I had to sell all of it. Our parents had many debts to pay off. There is nothing left but this empty house. As I have a wife and you have none, I will keep the house. By the way, you can keep our parents' dog and cat." The older brother had no use for these old, useless animals.

The younger brother trusted his brother and said nothing. So it was that the older brother took the house, the family fortune, the rice fields, and the oxen. For Tran there was only a small corn field in the hills near Stone Mountain and the tired dog and cat.

Tran bowed low to his brother and left for the field with his animals. Once there he looked around in despair. How was he going to plow the land? He had no horse, no ox, no donkey. The old dog and cat looked at Tran with curiosity. Finally, Tran attached the two

tired animals to his plow. Tran called, "Let's go, old friends! We must plow this field." The dog howled, the cat cried out, and the plow made a crooked path across the field. What a strange sight they were!

The Demon of Stone Mountain had been watching Tran and the animals. He couldn't believe what he saw. How funny they all looked! At first he smiled. Then he laughed loud and hard. His fat sides shook and his great stone mouth opened wide.

Scared by the loud noises coming from the mountain, Tran looked up. The young brother gave a cry of surprise. Inside the open mouth of the mountain was a beautiful sight. There were piles and piles of shining gold. Tran quickly climbed up the mountain and inside the mouth. There he filled his sack with gold. He escaped just in time. As soon as he jumped out, the mouth closed with a loud noise.

Tran was delighted with his good fortune. He spent the gold wisely. In the village, he paid builders to make him a house at the foot of Stone Mountain. He bought a rice field and two oxen. Satisfied, he was ready to live a fine life with his loyal dog and cat.

Hearing of his brother's great luck, the older brother was miserable. His heart was filled with greed and envy. One day he visited his younger brother. He asked him about his good fortune. The honest younger brother told him exactly what had happened.

The older brother's mind was filled with visions of gold. Planning greedily, he thought of a thousand ways to spend the mountain's fortune. The very next day the greedy brother took his wife and his two oxen carts to Stone Mountain. He was hoping to place huge amount of gold in the carts. From his brother's home, he borrowed the old dog and cat.

Quickly the older brother attached the tired dog and cat to the old plow. Imitating Tran's actions, he pushed the plow across the field. The dog howled, the cat cried out, and again the Demon Mountain laughed at the sight. His fat sides shook and his great stone mouth opened wide. Shining brightly inside was the fortune in gold.

The man and his wife rushed inside the mountain, carrying several sacks. They filled the first sack, then another, and yet one more. Still they were not satisfied.

By this time the Demon's humor had turned to anger. His smile changed into a frown. With a terrible noise his stone mouth came crashing shut. The greedy brother and his wife were closed inside.

Early the next morning, the younger brother came out of the house. He saw his dog and cat and the two empty oxen carts. That was all; there was no one or nothing more. Slowly, Tran looked up at the mountain. The Demon gave the brother a quick smile and a wink of the eye.

Comprehension

Match two parts to make a correct sentence about the story.

1. The greedy older brother mountain.
2. Tran had only shut inside.
3. When the Demon laughed, himself.
4. Tran filled a sack
5. The older brother tried
6. The Demon closed his mouth

A. to take too much gold from the

B. and the brother and wife were

C. wanted his parents' fortune for

D. with gold from the mountain.

E. Tran could see gold inside.

F. a corn field, an old dog and cat.

Deeper Understanding

Answer each question, either in a discussion with the class or in your own journal.

1. Why did the Demon get angry and close his mouth with the brother and wife inside?
2. Does the Demon like Tran? Use evidence from the story.
3. In the beginning of the story, Tran trusted his brother. Do you think he still trusts him at the end of the story? Explain.
4. Do you think Tran will try to rescue his brother and brother's wife? Why or why not?
5. Name one value that is respected in this story, and one value that is disliked. Choose among the following values:

friendliness	patriotism
honest effort	love
greed	bad temper

Literary Element

Theme

Theme is an important element in most literature. A theme is the main idea or concept of the selection. It is an idea that the writer wants the reader to remember. To find the theme, ask yourself the question, "What is the writer trying to tell me?"

- *What is this folktale saying about greed?*

- *What is the folktale saying about taking and using only what you need?*

BEYOND

Game

Play bingo with words from the story. Fold a piece of paper into sixteen equal parts. (Do this by folding the paper in half four times.) Write these words in different squares on the paper (but NOT in this same order): demon, funeral, greedy, fortune, debt, field, oxen, useless, despair, plow, curiosity, crooked, howl, envy, borrow, wink. Choose a bingo caller to call out the definition of the words until someone gets bingo.

Interview

Speak with someone who is from or has been to Vietnam. Ask about the land and the people. Share this information with the class.

Quiz

Divide into groups. Each group makes a test about Vietnam and the story. Use true/false questions, matching, multiple choice questions, etc. Then trade tests with other groups to answer.

Creative Project

Make a collage of "greed" and another of "honest effort." Find pictures from magazines and newspapers that give the idea of these words.

Writing Project

Write about an example of greed that you have seen or heard about. Give details about the person and exactly what he or she did that was greedy.

La Mocuana

Knowing the Area

"La Mocuana" is a Nicaraguan legend. Below you will find information about the geography, people, and history of Nicaragua.

Geography

Look at the map at the front of the book. Answer each question.

A. Nicaragua is in the area between North and South America. What is this area called?
B. What is the ocean to the west of Nicaragua?
C. What countries border Nicaragua?

Land and People

Complete each sentence with the correct word.

poet	**Central**	**Spanish**
Indian	**religion**	**write**

Nicaragua is the largest country in _____America. The country has a
                                              A
tropical forest, plains, and the largest lake in the area. The population is

mainly of mixed _____ and Spanish descent. The majority speak _____,
                    B   C
although some Nicaraguans speak English. Most of the people are Roman

Catholic in _____. Since 1979, the literacy rate has increased from fifty
               D
percent to eighty-seven percent. ("Literacy rate" means the number of

people who can read and _____.)
                           E

Nicaraguans favorite sport is baseball. A few of their players have made

it to the major leagues in the United States. One of Latin America's most famous writers was born in Nicaragua. Ruben Dario (1867–1916) was a

_____ who helped change modern Hispanic literature.
  F

History

Read the passage about the history of Nicaragua. Then complete the exercise that follows the passage.

Various Indian groups were the first people to live in Nicaragua. Some of the Indians had an advanced culture. Their artwork included ornaments of gold. Columbus landed in Nicaragua in 1502. Spain first founded colonies in Nicaragua in 1522. In that year a Spanish explorer, Gil Gonzalez de Avila, became friends with the Indian chief Nicarao. The country is now named for this chief. Nicaragua became independent of Spain in 1821. At that time it formed part of the Central American Federation. Then in 1838 Nicaragua became a republic.

In 1912 Nicaragua asked the U.S. for aid. The U.S. Marines occupied Nicaragua off and on until 1933. The powerful Somoza family ruled the country from 1937 to 1979. At that time, the Sandinista guerrillas forced somoza to leave the country. The Sandanistas ruled Nicaragua from 1979 until 1984. Then Daniel Ortega, one of the Sandinistas, was elected president and served until 1990. During Ortega's presidency, a group fought against the Sandinistas. This group, called the Contras, was given support by the United States.

Rewrite each scrambled sentence in the correct word order.

A. made objects / Nicaragua's / advanced Indian cultures / of gold
B. is named / after / Nicaragua / the / Nicarao / Indian chief
C. had colonies / in / Nicaragua / Spain / for / 300 years
D. broke away / in 1821 / and became / Nicaragua / from Spain / in 1838 / a republic
E. from 1933 to 1979 / the Somoza family / the government / controlled
F. from 1984 to 1990 / leader of the / Daniel Ortega / was president / Sandinistas / and

Getting Ready for the Folktale

Discussion

"La Mocuana" is a ghost story. Do you believe in ghosts? Why or why not?

A *cave* is an important part of this legend. As a class or in small groups, make a list of the things that you could find in a cave.

Vocabulary

*Look at the first picture in the story. Point to the Spanish **soldier**, the Indian **maiden**, the full **moon**, and the **lake**. In the next picture, point to the Indian maiden's **braid**, to the **cave**, and to the **bats**.*

THROUGH

This tragic legend tells of a young Indian maiden's love for a Spanish soldier.

LA MOCUANA

Once long ago in the land that is now Nicaragua there was a tribe of Indians. These people were excellent artisans. They made beautiful things with their hands. Cacique Nicarao was the chief of the Indians. He lived in a village with his people. Among his valuable possessions were ornaments of gold. But above all of his lovely belongings, his most prized possession was his daughter. She was called Nicaya. Her uncommon physical beauty was breathtaking. She was also known for her kindness and patience. Her inner beauty shone through her bright, black eyes.

At this time the Spanish came to the land of the Indians. Nicarao welcomed the men. To him, the light-skinned men were like gods. He invited the Spaniards to a celebration at his home. The finest food of the land was prepared for the men. One of the soldiers was named Diego. He was blond and handsome with eyes that were always laughing. His love for the ladies was well known among his friends. Diego lost no time in spotting Nicaya, the chief's daughter. Nicaya wore a long white dress. Flowers of bright colors were embroidered at the bottom of the skirt. Her long, black hair hung in a braid down to her knees. She looked into Diego's eyes, then quickly turned the other way.

The young captain walked over to Nicaya. "I am Diego," the young captain said to Nicaya. He took her fine hands in his own. "I know you cannot understand me. I don't know your language. But

still I must tell you that you are the most beautiful woman I have ever seen." Nicaya didn't comprehend the words, but she knew their meaning. Her cheeks blushed red with a sudden shyness.

"Nicaya, come here at once." Nicarao didn't like the look in the young man's eyes. Besides, he didn't want his daughter to fall in love with a stranger. The father was too late, however. Nicaya's heart was already lost to the handsome Spaniard with the smooth voice.

Diego was not soon to forget the Indian maiden, either. He became friends with a servant of Nicarao. Diego gave the servant presents, then made arrangements to meet secretly with the Indian maiden. One night during a full moon, Nicaya came to see Diego. They met by a small lake outside the village. The young woman's white dress shone in the bright moonlight. Her long, black hair hung loosely around her like a black cloud. Unbraided, her hair almost reached the ground.

"You are even more lovely than I remembered!" Diego touched the maiden's soft cheek with his hand. "I want you to be by my side." Diego had found someone to speak to the maiden. The man translated everything Diego said to Nicaya. "I want to marry you. I know your father won't like it, so we must escape at night in two weeks' time."

Without hesitation, the maiden agreed agreed to marry the young soldier. "We will need money to return to Spain. Bring a box filled with your father's gold," said Diego. Nicaya promised to get the gold.

"Two weeks will seem an eternity to me. Never forget my love for you," said Diego. He kissed Nicaya gently, then said good night.

It was the day before Nicaya was to leave with Diego. She was very nervous, but she knew she wanted to marry the soldier. Carefully she hid a box of gold in her room. Suddenly she heard sharp, loud noises and screams. What was wrong? Outside, she saw the Spanish soldiers running. They were killing her people with their guns. Blood was everywhere. The echo of the screams of children rang in Nicaya's ears.

"Nicaya! Come with me!" It was Diego riding towards her on his horse. He picked he up and placed her next to him. Away they rode, far from the screaming and dying people. Diego took Nicaya to the hills above the lake. He stopped in front of a dark cave. "Nicaya, I want you to stay here in this cave," said Diego. "I'm afraid the other soldiers might find you. They would kill or abuse you. Here you'll be safe."

Nicaya could say nothing. She was still in shock after seeing her people killed.

"Tell me where you hid the gold. Then I'll come back for you and we can go to Spain." He said the Indian word for *gold*. Nicaya drew a picture in the dirt. She pointed to where she had put the gold.

"Don't worry, my love." Diego kissed Nicaya good-bye and told her to enter the cave. Nicaya went inside. Then Diego moved three big, heavy rocks to block the entrance to the cave. "I'll see you soon!" Diego shouted as he rode down the hill.

Nicaya was long inside the dark cave. The air smelled bad. She could only see a little light coming through the cracks of the rocks. Above her was a strange noise. There were bats flying inside the cave. Nicaya started to shake with fear. Then she laid her head down on the ground and cried.

Diego rode back to the village. There were dead bodies everywhere. He looked in the spot where Nicaya had hid the gold. An empty box was all he could find. "That stupid girl!" Diego said to himself. "She can't even hide a box of gold! Someone has already found and taken the treasure." Diego was furious. He threw the box across the room. "She will be punished! I'm going to return home without her. There are lots of pretty women with rich fathers in Spain." Diego rode back to the soldiers' camp. The next day the ship left for Spain, carrying the soldiers and the Indians' gold.

Nicaya waited and waited for her young soldier. At first she was patient, knowing he would return. She drank water from a small stream in the cave. That night she slept very little. She could feel spiders crawling all over her. Sounds of unknown creatures were all around her.

During the day she found small plants growing in the cave to eat. Questions entered her mind. What if something had happened to Diego? Was he still alive? She tried desperately to move the rocks from the cave entrance. It was not possible.

Hours and then days passed. A terrible thought came to Nicaya. What if he had left her there to die?

Even today people speak of Nicaya. At night, some say they can still hear her cry out for her loved one. They tell stories that she walks the dark streets of Granada, a city in Nicaragua. They call her an Indian name, La Mocuana, because of her long hair. Wearing a black dress, she looks for young men. Her black hair hangs all around her, reaching the ground. Her face is covered by her long black hair. When she finds a handsome young man who has done wrong to his girlfriend, she pulls her hair aside. No one can describe the face of La Mocuana. That is because no one sees her face and lives to tell about it.

Comprehension

Tell whether each sentence is true or false.

1. Cacique Nacarao is the chief of the Indians.
2. Nicarao's most prized possession is his gold.
3. Diego is blond, handsome, and one of the Indian soldiers.
4. Nicaya, the chief's daughter, falls in love with Diego.
5. Diego and Nicaya will have a big Indian celebration when they marry.
6. Diego wants Nicaya to bring gold with her when they escape.
7. The Spanish soldiers kill the Indians with bows and arrows.
8. Diego takes Nicaya and hides her in a cave.
9. Diego finds the gold and takes it with him back to Spain.
10. Diego never returns to take Nicaya out of the cave.
11. Some say Nicaya still walks the streets of Granada, a city in Nicaragua.
12. Nicaya, called La Mocuana, is looking for handsome men who are nice to their girlfriends.

Deeper Understanding

Answer each question, either in a discussion with the class or in your own journal.

1. Why do you think the Spanish killed the Indians?
2. What probably happened to Nicaya in the cave?
3. Why does Nicaya's ghost still walk the streets of Granada?
4. How much of this legend do you know is true? (Look at the History exercise for more information.)
5. Name two traits from this legend that are disliked. Give an example of each from the legend. Choose from the following traits:

wisdom	laziness
cruelty	patience
greed	rudeness

Literary Element

Setting

The *setting* is the time and place of a story's action. Sometimes the setting is described in great detail. At other times, there may not be very much information about the setting of a story.

- *What is the time of the legend "La Mocuana"? (Look at the History section for more information.)*

- What are the three main places in the setting of this legend?
- Which place in the setting was described in most detail? Why do you think this place was described in detail?

BEYOND

Game

Work in pairs. Each partner finds eight words from the story that can be described in a picture. Then the first partner gives directions to draw the picture for the word. The partner does not tell the other the word; the other partner must guess what he/she is drawing. Take turns giving directions and drawing pictures.

Interview

Ask friends and family to describe their favorite ghost story. Report your findings to the class.

Creative Project

Imagine that "La Mocuana" is a movie. Make a poster advertisement for the movie. Include the title, a drawing, and comments about the story. (Look at a movie advertisement in the newspaper for an example.)

Writing Project

Write a ghost story. You can retell a story you have heard before. Or you can invent your own ghost story.

The Seeing Stick

Knowing the Area

"The Seeing Stick" is a Chinese folktale. Below you will find information about the geography, people, and history of China.

Geography

Look at the map in the front of the book. Answer each question.

A. What large country is to the north of China?
B. What ocean is to the east?
C. What continent is China on?

Land and People

Complete each sentence with the correct word.

| important | people | wheat |
| country | north | three |

The land of China has _____ main regions. The west is mostly desert,
                        A
the _____ has plains (flat land), and the south is mostly hills and valleys.
    B
Agriculture is still important to China. Some of the products include rice,

_____, and tea. China has the biggest population of any _____ in the world.
  C   D
There are over one billion _____.
                            E

China has been known for strong family relations. Now loyalty to the

government is very _____.
                   F

History

Read the passage about China. Then complete the exercise that follows the passage.

China is one of the world's oldest civilizations. The country was ruled by different dynasties for thousands of years. (A dynasty is a line of rulers from the same family.) During the Ming dynasty (1368–1644) the Great Wall was built in North China. It extends for more than 1,200 miles from the coast to the desert. Communists took control of the government after World War II. Mao Tse-Tung become the leader until he died in 1976. The government has tried to increase industry in the country. China is now open to foreign trade. In 1989 the students tried to get more democratic freedom. The government ended their efforts with violence.

Rewrite each scrambled sentence in the correct word order.

A. one / world's / civilizations / China / of / is / oldest / the
B. dynasties / China / ruled / different / was / by
C. leader / China's / Mao Tse-Tung / was / 1976 / until
D. foreign / open / China / is / to / trade
E. ended / students' / for / the / efforts / government / democracy

Getting Ready for the Folktale

Group Work

In groups, pair one word from list A with a word from list B. Then explain the association between each pair.

A	B
emperor	carve
magician	touch
knife	trick
clothes	ragged
blind	medicines
healer	fortune
stick	wood

Journal

Imagine that you suddenly went blind. Describe three things that you would miss seeing. Explain why.

THROUGH

This is a Chinese folktale of a blind princess.

THE SEEING STICK

In ancient China, there lived an emperor and his daughter. The emperor was wise and kind, and he had a long dark beard. They lived in the city of Peking, which was surrounded by strong walls.

The emperor's only daughter was named Hwei Ming. Her long black hair was held back with white ivory combs. She wore jade rings of brilliant green on her delicate fingers. Her clothes and tiny shoes were made of the finest silk.

However, these lovely things did not make Hwei Ming happy. The girl was blind and could not see her beautiful possessions.

Her father was sad for his daughter but did not cry. The day he became emperor he said he would cry no more. But he did make an offer of a fortune in jewels to the person who could help his daughter.

People came from near and far to try to win the fortune. A woman healer came to help the princess. The healer was short and round. She always had a wide smile on her face. The woman gave Hwei Ming many different medicines. Nothing helped. Finally the healer said, "Princess, I am so sorry. I cannot cure you." The woman's wide smile was replaced with a sad look.

Another day an evil magician came to the palace. The man was tall and thin. He never looked directly at anyone. Instead, his eyes were always racing around the room. "Ah, Princess, I am certain I can help you see!" The magician tried many tricks. He even gave her a magic drink. But the princess was still blind. At last he said angrily, "No one can ever help you!" The guards took him out of the palace.

One day an old man stopped by the city gates. The man's face showed the lines of time. He had gray hair and a gray beard. His clothes were old and ragged from his long travels. He had walked for many days to help the princess. He carried with him his long walking stick and his carving knife.

The two guards at the gate would not let the ragged old man enter. They said, "Go away, Grandfather! There is nothing for you here." One of the guards put his sword in the old man's face.

The old man touched each of the guard's faces. "So young," he said, "yet already so old." The old man sat down and started to carve his stick with his knife.

The guards were sorry they were unkind to an old man. "Grandfather, what are you doing?" asked one of the guards.

"I have a stick that sees," said the old man.

"That's nonsense!" said the guard. "Your stick can see no better than the emperor's blind daughter."

"Maybe, maybe not. Let me tell you about my travels." As the old man talked, he cut the golden piece of bamboo. He carefully carved pictures into his stick. On the stick was himself, the two guards, and the walls of Peking.

The guards were amazed by the pictures. "This is something the emperor would like to see," said one guard. "He admires beautifully made things."

The guards went to the palace. There they told the emperor about the man and his stick. Hwei Ming was sitting next to her father. "Oh, I wish I could see this wonderful stick!" she said.

"Let me show it to you," said the old man. "This is no ordinary stick, but a stick that sees."

"Nonsense!" said her father angrily.

But the princess asked, "A seeing stick?"

The old man touched the hair and face of the princess. Smiling, he pulled out his knife. As he told the princess about his travels, he carved people and objects into the bamboo. After each story, he placed the girl's delicate fingers on the stick.

"Feel the long hair of the princess on the stick," said the old man. "Now touch your own hair," he said. She did as he told her.

"Now feel the lines in this old man's face. Years of troubles and years of joy." He placed her fingers again on the stick. Then he held her hands to touch his face. The princess had not touched a person's face since she was a baby.

"Guards, come here!" she cried out. She touched the faces of the guards. Then she found them on the seeing stick.

Next Hwei Ming touched the face of her father. She felt a tear on his face. This was surprising, as the emperor had said he would cry no more.

"Father, now I want to know the city!" The emperor, his daughter, the old man, and the guard walked through the streets. Princess Hwei Ming touched the faces and clothes of the people as she passed. Finally she came to the walls of Peking. She felt the large, smooth stones.

"This is wonderful! Grandfather, please tell me another story." The voice of the princess was filled with laughter and happiness.

"Tomorrow I will," said the old man.

The old man told the princess many stories for as long as he lived. The emperor gave the man a fortune in jewels. However, the old man gave the jewels to the poor people of the city.

The princess said that she grew eyes on the ends of her fingers. At least this is what she told the blind children of the city. She showed them how to feel things with their hands.

The princess knew it was possible to see by touching.

As did all of the blind children of Peking.

As did the blind old man.

Comprehension

Tell whether each sentence is true or false.

1. In the beginning of the story, the princess was happy because of all of her beautiful things.
2. At first, the guards wouldn't let the old man enter the gates of Peking.
3. The old man showed the guards the pictures he carved into the wall.
4. The old man showed the princess how to see by touching.
5. The emperor gave the old man a fortune, and the old man kept it all for himself.
6. The princess didn't want to help the other blind children.
7. The old man with the seeing stick was also blind.

Deeper Understanding

Answer each question, either in a discussion with the class or in your own journal.

1. Why did the magician, the healer, and the old man want to help the princess? Compare the reasons.
2. Why did the emperor cry?
3. Do you think "the seeing stick" is a good name for the old man's stick? Explain your answer.
4. The reader finds out at the end of the story that the old man is blind. What clues are in the story that the old man is blind?
5. In this story, the blind princess learns to use her sense of touch to help her "see." Handicapped persons learn to depend on different ways to help themselves. Give other examples.
6. Name one value that is respected in this folktale and one value that is disliked. Choose from the following values:

anger	love of nature
disrespect of elders	peace
helpfulness	greed

Literary Element

Character

Characters are an important element in most literature. A character is a person in a story or drama. You can find out about a character in these ways: (1) by a description of the character; (2) by what the character says or does; (3) by the other characters' reactions to the character.

- *Write the phrase* old man *on a piece of paper and circle it. Then write down things you know about the old man from the description of him, from what he says or does, and how the other characters react to him.*

BEYOND

Game

Bring an object form home and place it in a bag. The others in your group will try to guess what it is by touching it only. They can ask you yes/no questions about the object.

Creative Project

Write a character poem about one of the characters in the story. Choose one of these characters: the emperor, Hwei Ming, the old man, the magician, or the healer.

Here is the format:
    Name of character
    three adjectives describing the personality of the character
    five words describing the appearance of the character
    seven words telling something the character said or did

For example:
    Peking guard
    Young, unkind, curious
    Carries a sword with him
    Took the old man to the emperor

Writing Project

Imagine that you are blind. Write about what you can learn using your sense of touch.

The Snow Maiden _____

Knowing the Area

"The Snow Maiden" is a story from the Soviet Union. Below you will find information about the geography, people, and history of the Soviet Union.

Geography

Look at the map in the front of the book. Answer each question.

   A. On what continent is the Soviet Union located?
   B. What ocean is to the east of the Soviet Union?
   C. Name three countries that border on the Soviet Union.

Land and People

Complete each sentence with the correct word.

cold	language	largest
people	spoken	fifteen

The Union of Soviet Socialist Republics (U.S.S.R.) is the _____
country in the world. It has the third-largest population in the world. The Soviet Union consists of _____ republics. The largest and most populated is the Russian Republic. Most of the U.S.S.R. has very _____ winters.

Russian is the official _____. More than one hundred other languages are also _____. There are 170 different ethnic groups. Officially there is no religion. But some _____ still practice a religion.

History

Read the passage about the Soviet Union. Then complete the exercise that follows the passage.

In the 400s, the Slavs came to Russia. Peter the Great was czar (ruler) from 1672 to 1725. He brought the ways of the west to Russia. Catherine the Great extended the territory of Russia during the 1700s. During this time, many poor Russians worked as serfs (slaves) for the rich. The serfs were liberated in 1861. In 1905, the Russian Revolution started. The people revolted because of poor economic and political conditions. In 1922, Russia joined with other surrounding republics to form a much larger country called the U.S.S.R. The U.S.S.R. was the worlds' first communist state. In communist states the economy is controlled by the government.

After World War II, the Soviet Union became a world power. In 1985 Mikhail Gorbachev became general secretary of the U.S.S.R. Communist Party. As leader, Gorbachev thas made changes in the government. He wanted to help the country's slow economy. He has also brough some democracy to Soviet politics. In 1987, Gorbachev met with the president of the U.S. at that time, Ronald Reagan, and agreed on a nuclear forces treaty.

Rewrite each scrambled sentence in the correct word order.

   A. brought / Peter the Great / Western ways / Russia / to
   B. started / Russian Revolution / the / economic and political / because of / problems.
   C. became / the first / the U.S.S.R. / communist / in the / world / state
   D. became / world / the U.S.S.R. / power / World War II / after / a
   E. has made / Gorbachev / as leader / in the / changes / government
   F. slow economy / he / wanted / the country's / to help

Getting Ready for the Folktale

Group Work

"The Snow Maiden" is a Russian story about a girl made of snow. In a small group, write down words that relate to snow. Think of different nouns, verbs, and adjectives.

Vocabulary

The story talks about Heaven. Where is "Heaven"? What does Heaven represent?

Journal

In "The Snow Maiden" a man and wife want a child very much. They are sad because they have no children. Write about something you wanted very much and couldn't have. How did you feel?

This Russian story tells of a couple's wish for a child.

The Snow Maiden

Once long ago there was a simple farmer named Ivan and his wife Marousha. They loved each other very much and led a good life. Still, they were very sad. Their sorrow was because they had no children. Hour after hour, they would watch their neighbors' children having fun. They loved to hear the boys and girls laughing and playing.

It was winter time, and the first big snow had fallen. The trees and ground were covered in pure white. The world became a magic wonderland. Early in the morning, the children ran out to play. They threw snowballs at each other and jumped in the deep snow. Then they began to make a giant snow man. Ivan and Marousha enjoyed watching the children play.

Suddenly Ivan said, "Those children are having so much fun. Why don't we build ourselves a snowman?"

Marousha smiled happily. "What fun! But why build a big snowman? Let's make ourselves a snow child. We can pretend it is our own daughter."

Ivan agreed. The husband and wife went outdoors.

Outside their small wooden house, they began to make a child of snow. They carefully made a small body with little feet and hands. Next they rolled a small ball for the head.

A neighbor was walking by. "Good day! What are you doing, my friends?"

"We are making a snow child," answered Ivan.

"Then Heaven bless you!" replied the neighbor.

"How nice. The help of Heaven is good to have," said Marousha.

The two spent a long time forming the face. They used coal for the eyes and formed a delicate nose and chin.

At last the two stood back to admire their work. Then, to their amazement, the little snow maiden moved! Warm breath came from her lips. She had the most beautiful brown eyes. Her lips, the color of a rose, curved in a charming smile.

"What is this?" cried Ivan.

The maiden shook her head and snow fell from her lovely

brown hair. She moved her little arms and legs like a real child.

"Ivan!" cried Marousha. "Heaven has answered our prayers." The woman hugged the child and kissed her warmly.

"We will call you Vasilisa," said Marousha. The woman's face was covered with tears of joy. She hugged her husband. He was so happy he couldn't speak.

The little house, filled with sadness before, became a place full of life and joy. The other children came to play with the little snow maiden. They spent hours singing and talking to her.

The little snow girl was very clever. She learned everything quickly. Her voice was the music of silver bells. She was loving and obedient to her parents. All the neighborhood loved her dearly. She spent long hours playing in the snow. She could make beautiful things out of snow with her hands.

Day after day her parents watched her. "Heaven has given us great joy in our old age," said Marousha.

"We have much to be thankful for," agreed Ivan.

As always, the cold days of winter came to an end. The spring sun came out behind gray clouds. The snow disappeared and green grass grew high.

The other children sang happy songs of spring. They ran outside to play in the warm sun. Only the snow maiden stayed inside. She hid behind the window curtain, looking sad.

Marousha touched the child's brown hair. "Are you ill? You seem unhappy."

"Don't worry, Mother. I just don't feel like going outside."

Spring melted away the last of the snow. Flowers appeared

everywhere. Their garden was a rainbow of color. The birds in the forest sang a pure song. All the world was happy, except for the poor snow maiden.

She only went out in the late afternoon. Even then she was a timid flower, hiding under trees. She was most happy during the cool nights. Even a storm made her smile. Then, when the sun reappeared, she would begin to cry.

Summer came and it was almost time for the Feast of Saint John. The snow maiden's friends came to her house.

"Please come with us, Vasilisa. We're going to pick berries and flowers. We want to be ready for the Feast of Saint John," said her friends.

"No, I can't. I mustn't go outside," said Vasilisa. She turned her head away in fear.

"Go on, dear child. Look after her, children. You know how much I love her." The mother wanted her to play, although she also felt fear.

In the forest the children picked wild flowers. They ran around singing on the beautiful warm summer day. Each wore a crown of flowers. Only Vasilisa was unhappy. She sat sadly under a tree.

"Follow us, Vasilisa! Come run and dance, too!" the children shouted.

As the children ran, they heard a soft cry. They looked behind them and saw only a pool of water under the tree. The snow maiden was nowhere to be seen.

They called out her name. There was no answer.

"Where can she be? Maybe she went home," said the children. They went to her house, but Vasilisa wasn't there.

Everyone in the village looked day and night for the girl. They couldn't find her anywhere.

Marousha's heart broke into a million pieces. Ivan sat in his chair sadly, saying nothing. Days and months passed by.

It was fall and the days grew shorter. When the evening was cool, they thought they heard the girl's voice in the wind. "I hear our daughter's voice! I know it is our little girl!" cried out Marousha.

"Wait for winter, my wife," said Ivan. "Perhaps, when the snow returns, she will come back to us."

Comprehension

Match two parts to make a correct sentence about the story.

1. The man and woman were sad because
2. The girl made of snow
3. The little girl was clever,
4. When spring came
5. In the summer the girl
6. The little girl gave a cry
7. The children saw only
8. The man and woman hope that

A. went to the forest with her friends.
B. and then disappeared.
C. the girl wanted to stay inside.
D. turned into a live little girl.
E. the girl will return in the winter.
F. a pool of water under the tree.
G. loving, and obedient.
H. they didn't have a child.

Deeper Understanding

Answer each question, either in a discussion with the class or in your own journal.

1. Who or what do you think changed the snow child into a live girl?
2. Why do you think the little girl doesn't like spring or summer?
3. Why do you think the mother felt afraid before the little girl went to play in the forest?
4. What do you think happened to the little girl in the forest?
5. Do you predict the little girl will return in the winter? Why or why not?
6. Name two values that are respected in this story. Give examples. Choose among the following values:

love	freedom
cooperation	selfishness
jealousy	obedience

Literary Element

Metaphor

A *metaphor* is a figure of speech that makes a comparison between two different things.

Example from the story: "Her lips, the color of a rose, curved in a charming smile." In this example, the girl's lips are compared to the red of a rose.

Match two parts to form a metaphor from the story.

1. The world became a	A. rainbow of color.
2. Her voice was the	B. hiding under trees.
3. Their garden was a	C. into a million pieces.
4. She was a timid flower,	D. magic wonderland.
5. Marousha's heart broke	E. music of silver bells.

BEYOND

Game

Play a memory/speaking game with the whole class. The first person says something you can do in winter. Each person who follows has to repeat what was said before, and add something new about what you can do in winter. The one who can remember everything that is said wins.

Research

Find out about the holiday from the story called the Feast of Saint John. Why is it celebrated? When is it celebrated? Who celebrates this holiday? What activities occur on this day?

Creative Project

Make a metaphor poster. Write down the first part of a possible metaphor, such as "Friendship is _____." "Love is _____." "Fear is _____." Then find one or more picture that illustrates your choice. Paste the picture(s) on the poster. Complete the metaphor by describing what is in the picture(s). For example, "Fear is a dark, empty street with no lights on and not a person in view."

Writing Project

Write a play based on the story of "The Snow Maiden." Make a list of characters. Use a narrator to help tell the story. Then act out the play.

Urashima Taro _____

Knowing the Area

"Urashima Taro" is a Japanese folktale. Below you will find information about the geography, people and history of Japan.

Geography

Look at the map in the front of the book. Answer each question.

   A. What continent is Japan on?
   B. What ocean is to the east of Japan?
   C. Name four countries that are near Japan.

Land and People

Complete each sentence with the correct word.

poems	people	islands
universities	Shintoism	four	literature

    In the country of Japan, there are four major islands and many smaller ones. Around eighty percent of the _____ are mountainous. There are more

                  A
than 190 active volcanoes, and earthquakes are frequent. The population is dense, which means many _____ live in a small amount of land. Buddhism

                    B
and _____ are the main religions. Education is very important to the

    C
Japanese. Students compete to attend the colleges and _____.

                                           D

    A love of nature is important to the Japanese. This love is often seen through the arts. Paintings and _____, such as haiku poems, often describe

                        E
nature. Various holidays celebrate the _____ seasons.

                                  F

History

Read the passage about Japan. Then complete the exercise that follows the passage.

The Ainus, the original people of Japan, lived in the area since the year 4000 B.C. Invaders from Asia forced the Ainus into the north. (There are still a few Ainus in Japan today.) In the year 200 B.C. the Yamato dynasty united the country. Their religion formed the basis of Shintoism. Buddhism came from Korea. Shoguns (military dictators) ruled from 1192 to 1867. The Emperor Meiji (1867–1912) introduced ideas from the West. Japan became a world power in the 1900s. During World War II Japan joined forces with Germany. Both countries fought against the Allies, which included the countries of the U.S., Britain, and the U.S.S.R. Japan surrendered after the United States dropped atomic bombs on the cities of Hiroshima and Nagasaki in 1945.

Today Japan is again a world power. It is also an industrial giant. Exports from Japan include electronic equipment, ships, and cars.

Rewrite each scrambled sentence in the correct word order.

A. the Ainus / in Japan / for 6000 years / the first people / have lived
B. united Japan / in 200 B.C. / dynasty / the Yamato
C. called shoguns / ruled Japan / military dictators / 600 years / for
D. introduced / Emperor Meiji / ideas / the West / from / (1867–1912)
E. Japan / in World War II / after / the United States / surrendered / dropped atomic bombs
F. a world power / today / and industrial / Japan / giant / is

Getting Ready for the Folktale

Journal

In the story "Urashima Taro," the young man explores under the ocean. Would you like to explore the ocean? Why or why not?

Group Work

The Japanese have a love of nature. In small groups, make a list of the things you like most in nature.

Vocabulary

*Look at the pictures in the story. In the first one point to the **fisherman**, his **boat**, and the **sea turtle**. In the second one point to the **princess**, the **seahorses**, and the **coral**.*

This is a Japanese folktale about a man who finds great happiness under the sea.

Urashima Taro

Urashima Taro once lived in a small fishing village near the sea. During spring time the mountains behind the village were brilliant pink with cherry blossoms. During the summer the golden sun warmed the beaches of the village. Autumn brought fog, making it difficult for boats to find their way. But even the cold winter wind didn't stop the fishermen from going out to fish.

Every morning the boy Urashima Taro went to the sea with his father and brothers. One day, however, Taro stayed in the village to help his mother and grandmother. That afternoon a terrible storm roared in from the sea. After the storm was over, the boats came in slowly. Three boats did not return. The Urashima boat was one of the three that never came back.

Now Taro was the only man in the Urashima family. He knew he was no longer a boy. His days of sadness began.

The others called Taro the quiet one. Often Taro would walk alone along the peaceful beach. Once the children saw Taro climb a dangerous cliff to save a bird. Taro often helped animals in trouble on the beach.

On one of his walks, Taro saw some children tormenting a giant sea turtle. The turtle had turned on its back and the boys were beating him with sticks. Taro shouted at the children to stop. One look at Taro's angry face and the children ran off. The sea turtle went back into the sea and swam away.

A year passed. Taro found peace in nature, but he found no happiness for himself. One late afternoon, Taro was fishing when he heard a strange voice. "Urashima Taro!" The young man looked and saw the old sea turtle swimming next to the boat. "Do you remember how you helped me last year? I want to return the kindness. I told the Sea Princess, the daughter of the Dragon King, about you. She wants you to visit her in the castle under the water. No human eyes have ever seen this castle before."

Urashima Taro loved the sea and was excited to find out what was below. He climbed on the turtle's back. Deeper and deeper into the blue-green water swam the turtle and Taro. The young man could hardly believe the beauty under the ocean. Fish of every color

swam past him. The two went through a long, dark tunnel. At the end of the tunnel was an exquisitely beautiful castle. The palace sat on pure white sand in the midst of yellow and pink coral.

Taro walked through the doors of the castle. Standing before him was a woman more lovely than any that walk the earth. Her hair was blacker, her eyes were browner, and her lips were redder than any colors Taro had seen before. "Urashima Taro, you are welcome to my home." The Sea Princess smiled at him. She took Taro to eat in a huge room. Delicious food was placed on the table. Small purple fish swam everywhere. Mermaids danced for him. Little crabs moved in tune to the music. But the most lovely sight of all was the dancing Princess. Her movements were like waves of water. As she smiled at Taro, he lost his heart to her forever.

Urashima Taro and the Princess spent time without end together. She showed him all the wonders of the world below the sea. They swam on giant seahorses to explore the amazing sights.

Time passed. How long Taro did not know, as there was no way to measure time under the sea. One day he began to think about home. "Dear Princess, I am worried about my mother and grandmother. They are alone with no one to care for them. I must go back to visit them awhile."

"I was hoping you would stay here always. I do understand, however," said the princess. "But first I want to show you something." The Princess led him to a castle room with four doors. "These are the doors of your life. They are for all men, but not for us under the sea."

The first door was marked Spring. As Taro opened the door, the delicate smell of cherry blossoms met him. He felt sad, though,

knowing that the blossoms don't last. As he opened the Summer door, the smells of delicious fruits filled the air. Again he felt sad, knowing that fruit, once eaten, is gone. The next door opened to the warm browns and gold of Autumn. "This view is beautiful, but the colors come and go quickly," Taro said to the Princess. The last door opened to a scene of mountains and trees covered with white snow. The air was very cold. "Here I feel at peace," said Taro.

"Before you go, take this box." The Princess handed Taro an elegant box carved out of coral. "I am giving you a precious gift to show my love for you. It holds a gift never held by man before. Keep it close to you always, but never open it."

Urashima Taro climbed on the turtle's back and returned to his home. To his surprise, the land and houses were different. A tall tree stood in the place where his house had been. Villagers came up to talk to him. "Who are you? Where are you from?" they asked.

"I am Urashima Taro. I am from this village."

They shook their heads. No one knew the name. Then an old man spoke. "I remember that name! My grandfather told me a story about Urashima Taro. He was a young fisherman who drowned. But this happened three hundred years ago."

Taro couldn't believe it, but he knew all was changed. Sadly, he walked along the beach. His mother, grandmother, and his home were gone. Only the sea was still the same. Taro felt a grat longing to see the Princess again. Maybe the box would help him return to her.

Forgetting the Princess's warning, he opened the lid. Out came the secrets from behind the four doors. He smelled the flowers of spring and the fruit of summer. Around him were the colors of autumn and the cold winds of winter. At the same time he began to shake. His hair turned white and his skin became old. As he fell to the ground, a quiet peace came over him.

Today the villagers still tell the tale of the young man who looked for happiness under the sea.

Comprehension

Match two parts to form a correct sentence about the story.

Effects	Causes
1. The boy Taro was sad	A. because they were in love.
2. Taro helped animals	B. because he opened the box.
3. The turtle took Taro under the sea	C. because his father and brothers died in a storm.
4. Taro and the Prince spent time together	D. because he wanted to see the Princess again.
5. The Princess gave Taro a gift	E. because it was three hundred years later.
6. Taro's home had changed	F. because he was going back home.
7. Taro opened the box	G. because he wanted to reward Taro.
8. Taro became old	H. because he loved animals and nature.

Deeper Understanding

Answer each question, either in a discussion with the class or in your own journal.

1. What did the Princess's box with the four seasons represent?
2. What happened to Taro when he opened the box?
3. Do you think Taro died in peace? How do you know?
4. Did Taro find happiness? Explain.
5. Do you think Taro really wanted to live forever? Explain.
6. Name two values that are respected in this story. Choose from the following values:

trust	love of nature
loyalty	helpfulness
wisdom	hard work

Literary Element

Symbol

A *symbol* is something that stands for or represents something else. For example, a flag is a symbol that represents its country.

In the story "Urashima Taro," there are many symbols. Match the symbol with what it represents.

1. the Princess' gift
2. Spring
3. Summer
4. Autumn
5. Winter
6. the sea kingdom

A. early years in life
B. death
C. middle years in life
D. paradise
E. old age
F. eternal life

BEYOND

Game

In a small group, find ten vocabulary words from the story. Then each student gets a copy of a world map. Mark ten countries in the world, including Japan, that you would like to visit. Each student takes turns using the vocabulary words correctly in a sentence. At each correct answer, you mark off part of your journey on your map.

Research

Find a newspaper or magazine article about Japan. Share the article in small groups or with the class. Decide what is the main idea of the article. List any new things you learned about Japan.

Creative Project

Divide into small groups. Each group chooses once scene from the story to illustrate. Draw large pictures to post on the bulletin board in the correct sequence.

Writing Project

A haiku poem is a popular form of verse from Japan. Usually a scene from nature is described. Sometimes the scene is a symbol for a feeling or an idea. The poem has seventeen syllables and three lines (five syllables, seven syllables, five syllables). Write a haiku about one of the four seasons—spring, summer, autumn, or winter. Here is an example:

SPRING
A strong spring wind blows
Among the cherry blossoms.
Everywhere—pink rain.

𝕿he Three Wishes _____

Knowing the Area

"The Three Wishes" is a Hungarian folk tale. Below you will find information about the geography, people, and history of Hungary.

Geography

Look at the map in the front of the book. Answer each question.

    A. On what continent is Hungary located?
    B. What countries border Hungary?
    C. Is Hungary in the Eastern or Western part of Europe?

Land and People

Complete each sentence with the correct word listed below.

music	**lakes**	**speak**
poetry	**capital**	**wheat**

Hungary has low plains, forests, and _____. The Danube River goes
                                A
through Hungary. Most of the people are Magyars; they _____ Magyar
                                B
(Hungarian). About half of the population lives in cities. The largest city is
Budapest, the _____. Leading crops include corn and _____.
           C   D

Hungarians greatly enjoy music, _____, and the theater. A person who
                                E
plays native folk music is called a gypsy. Magyar folk _____ has been used by
                                            F
famous European composers in their works.

History

Read the passage about Hungary. Then complete the exercise that follows the passage.

The Magyars came to Hungary in A.D. 896 They were a tribe from Asia and were fierce fighters. In the eleventh century King Stephen I, the first king, brought Christianity to Hungary. In 1867 the country was part of Austria-Hungary. After World War II the country was occupied by Russia. By 1949 the country was communist. In 1956 there was a revolution against communism. Soviet forces defeated the revolutionaries.

Since 1968, their economic system has moved away from communism. In 1989 the Soviet Union began to lose its control over countries in Eastern Europe. As a result, Hungary began to move towards democracy.

Rewrite each scrambled sentence in the correct word order.

A. from Asia / in 896 / the Magyars / came to / Hungary
B. brought / King Stephen I / in the eleventh century / Christianity / to Hungary
C. became / communist / Hungary / by 1949
D. defeated / in 1956 / Soviet forces / Hungarian revolutionists
E. Hungary / towards democracy / in recent times / to move / has begun

Getting Ready for the Folktale

Journal

The story "The Three Wishes" is about a man and his wife and the three wishes they make. If you had one wish, what would it be?

Discussion

Tell about other stories you know in which the characters had wishes. Did they have problems with their wishes?

Vocabulary

*Look at the first picture in this story. Point to the **lady** and point to her **carriage**. Is the carriage higher or lower than the man's **waist**? Now draw a picture of a long **sausage** cooking in a **frying pan** in a **fire**. The fire is in a **chimney** inside a **house**. (You are drawing a scene from the story.)*

THROUGH

This Hungarian folktale is about a couple's chance to change their lives.

THE THREE WISHES

Once upon a time there was a couple who lived in a forest. They loved each other very much. Still, they argued all the time. They fought because they were poor and had no money. Instead of working hard to make money, they argued.

"Husband, why are you sitting by the fire? Go out and cut down wood in the forest!" shouted the wife.

"I am resting," said the husband. "I am too tired to work. You yelled at me all night and I couldn't sleep."

The old dog lying on the floor covered its head. The arguing hurt its ears.

"Stop yelling all of the time! Why don't you cook and sew? You have work to do yourself!" shouted the husband.

"How can I sew with you in the way? And you know there is nothing in the house to cook!" yelled the woman.

The man had to escape the fighting. He went out to the forest, taking the dog with him.

It was a clear, cool autumn day. It was time for the farmers to prepare the grapes to make wine. In the distance the man saw something unusual. A carriage was stuck in the muddy road. This was no ordinary carriage, however. It was a beautiful golden carriage. Four fine black horses were attached to it. To the man's surprise, the little carriage was no higher than his waist. He looked inside and

saw a pretty little woman. All dressed in gold, the woman was no bigger than a doll.

"Please, sir," spoke the woman. "Can you help me? My carriage is stuck in the mud. I don't want to get out and make my dress dirty."

"Are you an evil spirit?" asked the man. He thought about running away.

"Oh, no!" laughed the small woman. Her laughter was like the music of miniature bells. "I am certainly not evil. Indeed, if you help me, I will give you a reward."

The man thought a moment. Perhaps the woman would give him some money. With a little effort, he pushed the carriage out of the mud.

The little woman smiled happily. "Thank you so much! At last I'm free. Now, are you a rich man?"

"Oh, no," answered the man. "My wife and I are certainly the poorest for miles around."

"That can change," said the lady. "I will give your wife three wishes." In an instant the lady and her carriage disappeared from view.

The man could not believe it. He hurried home to tell his wife.

After hearing the story, the woman said, "Well, she made a fool of you! How can you believe her?"

"I'm sure she was a magic fairy. Now, wish for something, my wife," said the husband.

"Very well. But I doubt anything will happen," said the wife. "I'm hungry. I wish for some sausage to cook on our fire." Instantly there was a loud noise. A frying pan fell down the chimney. In it was a long sausage. It was big enough to feed ten men.

"Wonderful!" exclaimed the man. "We will be more clever with our next two wishes. We can ask for money to buy two cows, two horses, and a pig." The man took a closer look at the sausage. Accidentally, he knocked the frying pan. Into the fire went the sausage.

"You clumsy man! What have you done to the sausage?" cried out the woman. "I wish the sausage would grow onto your nose!"

No sooner said than the sausage was out of the fire and hanging on the husband's nose. The end of the long sausage touched the man's toes.

"Foolish woman, what have you done?" yelled the man. "Now our second wish is gone. And look at my nose!"

At first they tried to pull the sausage off his nose. He pulled and

she pulled until his nose was almost pulled off. Yet the sausage was still stuck on his nose.

"Let me try to cut off the sausage," said the woman.

"Goodness, no!" shouted the man. "You will be cutting off a part of my nose. You must wish the sausage back in the pan."

"But what about the cows and the horses and the pig?" cried the woman.

"Well, I can't walk around like this all my life. And do you want to kiss me with a sausage on my nose?" asked the man.

The woman had to laugh through her tears. She made the third wish and the sausage was in the pan again. They were just as poor as before the wishes.

After eating the delicious meal, the two talked.

"Husband, we argue too much. As a result, we lost our three wishes," said the woman.

"You're right, my wife. We must try to do better." The man and wife kissed and promised not to fight.

After that moment, they argued no more. In time they earned cows, horses, and a pig by working hard. They made their own wishes come true.

Comprehension

Tell whether each sentence is true or false.

1. There once was a couple who lived in a village in Hungary.
2. The husband and wife didn't love each other.
3. The man and woman fought because they had no money.
4. They argued but still they worked hard most of the time.
5. There was nothing in their house to cook.
6. The man saw a golden carriage with four fine black horses.
7. The lady in the carriage gave the man three wishes because he helped her.
8. The first wish was for a lot of food to eat.
9. The woman next wished for the sausage to be on the end of the man's nose.
10. The last wish was for cows, horses, and a pig.
11. The man and woman promised not to fight any more.

Deeper Understanding

Answer each question, either in a discussion with the class or in your own journal.

1. Why do you think the woman wished for the sausage to be on the end of her husband's nose?
2. How did the three wishes help the husband and wife?
3. Name one value that is respected in this folktale and one value that is disliked. Choose from the following values:

fighting	hard work
love of nature	trust
selfishness	lying

Literary Element

Climax

The *climax* of the story is the turning point in the action of the story. The end of the story is affected by what happens in the climax.

- *What is the climax of the story "The Three Wishes"?*

- *The climax in this story determines what happens in the end. How would the story have ended differently if the wife had made a different last wish?*

BEYOND

Game

In small groups, find ten difficult words from the story. Make cards the size of playing cards from cardboard. For each vocabulary word, write the word on one card and draw a picture representing the word on another card. Then play concentration with the vocabulary cards. (Turn the cards over and try to match the word with its picture.)

Survey

Ask family and friends what they would wish for if they had three wishes. Share the results with the class.

Creative Project

Divide into small groups. Use the information your group gained from the survey of the wishes people want. Classify the wishes into different categories. Then make a graph of the wish categories and the amount in each category.

Writing Project

Write an essay about your choices if you had three wishes. Give reasons for each wish.

Pecos Bill

INTO

Knowing the Area

"Pecos Bill" is a folktale from southwest United States. Below you will find information about the geography, people, and history of the United States.

Geography

Look at the map in the front of the book. Answer each question.

   A. On what continent is the United States located?
   B. What country is south of the United States? What country is to the north?
   C. What two states are separate from the main part of the United States?

Land and People

Complete each sentence with the correct word.

religious	excellent	deserts
Grand population	people	snow

The United States is the fourth-largest country in the world in both area and _____. The climate and land vary greatly across the United States.
<u>A</u>
There are _____, high mountains, flat plains, and subtropical land. The
<u>B</u>
climate includes area that receive a lot _____ and other areas of mild winters.
<u>C</u>
There are many beautiful national parks in the U.S., such as the _____
<u>D</u>
Canyon.

There are also a mixture of ethnic groups in the United States. People from all over the world have come to live there. Many came for political and _____ freedom. The American Indians, the first _____ in America, live in
<u>E</u> <u>F</u>
all states. The U.S. is known for its _____ system of higher education.
<u>G</u>

History

Read the passage about the United States. Then complete the exercise that follows the passage.

There were Indians living all over North America by the year 6000 B.C. Beginning in 1565, settlers came to the area from Spain, England, and France. Problems arose among the thirteen English colonies in North America. The settlers fought against the British in the Revolutionary War (1775–1783). As a result, the United States became an independent country. In 1789, George Washington became the first president of the U.S. Originally there were thirteen states in the eastern part of the U.S. Following treaties in the 1800s with Spain and France, the U.S. extended across the continent. The state of Texas became part of the U.S. in 1945. Today there are fifty states, including Alaska and Hawaii.

In the 1900s the U.S. became a world power. Its military forces helped end World War II.

Rewrite each scrambled sentence in the correct word order.

A. first / were / inhabitants / Indians / the / in North America
B. settlers / after 1565 / from Spain, England, and France / came to / North America
C. was / the / president / of / the original thirteen / first / states / George Washington
D. are / fifty states / there / now / United States / in the
E. helped / to / the U.S. / end / World War II

Getting Ready for the Folktale

Group Work

The story of "Pecos Bill" takes place in the state of Texas. Texans are very proud of their state. Find Texas on a U.S. map. How does Texas compare in size to the other states? Relate any examples you know about proud Texans.

Brainstorm

"Pecos Bill" is a story of an imaginary Texan cowboy. In a group, write down everything you know about cowboys. Why are cattle important to cowboys?

Discussion

"Pecos Bill" is an example of a tall tale. Tall tales are funny, exaggerated stories about real or invented people. Why do you think people like to tell tall tales?

Vocabulary

Look at the pictures in the story. Find the picture of Pecos Bill. Point to the **mountain lion** *and to the* **lasso** *made from a* **rattlesnake**. *Describe a rattlesnake. Find the picture of Slue-Foot Sue. Point to the* **bustle** *on the back of her skirt. The horse is* **bucking**. *What does that mean?*

THROUGH

In the old West, the cowboys loved to tell tall tales, especially about other cowboys.

Pecos Bill

Pecos Bill was born in Texas. From the beginning he did his best to live up to the honor of being a Texan. Bill's mother knew he was special. She took milk from a mountain lion to feed him. She also gave him a hunting knife to cut his teeth on. When Bill was a year old, Bill's brother ran up to his father in the field. "Hurry! There's a mountain lion in the cabin! And Bill's all alone with him!"

"Well," said the father. "That fool lion better not expect help from me!" When the father came home later that day, Bill was quite busy. He was cooking up lion steaks for the family.

One day Bill's father decided to move. "Too many people here. New neighbors moved in fifty miles from us. Let's go to west Texas." Just after the family wagon crossed the Pecos River, Bill fell out of the wagon. There were a dozen children in Bill's family. With so many others, it was four weeks before anyone realized Bill was gone.

Bill crawled around in the desert for a while. At last he saw a friendly pack of coyotes. First he showed them he was boss. Then he let them teach him everything they knew. He ran with the coyotes on moonlit nights. He slept with them in their rock dens. In the evenings, he and the coyotes howled a song to the stars.

These were happy days for Bill. After eight years with them, he believed he was a coyote, too. That's why he had such a hot argument with a cowboy one day. That cowboy was sure surprised to see a ten-year-old boy making noises like a coyote.

First the cowboy threw Bill a piece of tobacco. Bill liked it, so he didn't bite the man. Then the cowboy spent three days teaching Bill to talk like a human. After that he spent three more days telling

Bill he was a human, not a coyote.

"I sure am a coyote! I can howl the moon down from the sky. And I can run faster than a deer," argued Bill.

"All Texans can howl. But do you have a coyote's bushy tail?" asked the cowboy.

Bill looked around. He was surprised to see he didn't have a coyote's tail. "Well, maybe I lost it somewhere."

"No, siree. Shoot, you're a human being from top to bottom. Come be a cowboy like us," said the cowboy.

"I must be human, then. And I guess I'd best run with my own kind." Bill sadly told his coyote friends good-bye. He thanked them for all they had done. Then, riding on his mountain lion, he joined the cowboy. On the way they saw a big rattlesnake. The cowboy quickly rode off, but Bill grabbed the snake with his hands. He whipped the snake around and around until it was thirty feet long. Then he made a lasso with the snake. On his way to the ranch, he caught several animals with the snake rope.

"I never saw anybody catch animals like that with a snake," said the cowboy in surprise.

"That's because I just invented the lasso," responded Bill.

That wasn't the end of it. Bill made his home with the cowboys at the ranch. Then he invented all kinds of things to make the cowboy's life easier. He showed them how to rope cattle and how to take the cattle to market. He also taught the cowboys how to sing cowboy songs. "I used to love howling at the moon. I'll make up some tunes to sing while we're riding at night." Even Hard-Nose Hal cried at the beauty of Bill's songs. Pecos Wrote all the best cowboy songs, like "Home on the Range" and "Git Along Little Doggies."

Bill was a big hero, but he wanted more to life. One day he found what he was looking for. He was walking near the Rio Grande when he saw a huge catfish jump out of the water. On its back was a pretty, brown-haired girl.

"Hey, look at Slue-Foot Sue ride that fish!" cried out another cowboy. Pecos Bill felt his heart go up to his head, down to his feet, and back home again. He knew this was the girl for him. He jumped into the water and grabbed Sue off the fish. "You're the girl I want to marry!" She agreed. She knew at once that he was the strongest, smartest cowboy in Texas.

Bill had a powerful horse named Widow Maker. He told Sue that she must never ride his horse. Right after the wedding, Sue jumped on Widow Maker. There she sat in her lovely wedding dress with its big bustle in back. But Widow Maker wouldn't take any rider except Bill. Right away the horse bucked and threw Slue-Foot

Sue high in the air. She went up and up until she flew right over the end of the new moon. Then, after a long time, she came down to earth. She landed on her skirt bustle. This made her bounce right up to the moon again. After several trips she called out to Bill. "Please, honey, won't you help me stop?"

"Oh, my pretty coyote, why didn't you listen to me?" asked Bill.

"I promise I'll listen to you from now on!" she called out. She was just about ready to hit the earth for the thirteenth time. Just in time, Bill lassoed her down. She kept on bouncing for awhile. Bill, though, kept a tight hold on the rope. Finally she stopped.

You'll be glad to know that Slue-Foot Sue and Pecos Bill had a fine life. No one knows how Pecos Bill died, or if he died. Next time you are in Texas, go out late at night. Listen to the coyotes howl at the moon. And realize that maybe Bill is singing right along with them.

Comprehension

Match two parts to make a correct sentence about the story.

1. Pecos Bill was born	A. and was thrown off Bill's horse.
2. As Bill's family crossed the Pecos River,	B. how to run and howl at the moon.
3. The coyotes taught Bill	C. out of a rattlesnake
4. After eight years with the coyotes,	D. in the state of Texas.
5. Bill made a rope	E. to make a cowboy's life easier.
6. Bill invented many things	F. Slue-Foot Sue.
7. Bill fell in love and married	G. Bill fell out of the wagon.
8. Sue didn't listen to Bill	H. Bill joined a group of cowboys.
9. Maybe even today Bill still	I. howls at the moon with the coyotes.

Deeper Understanding

Answer each question, either in a discussion with the class or in your own journal.

1. Was Bill's father worried about Bill's being alone with a mountain lion? Why or why not?
2. What evidence did the cowboy use to show Bill he wasn't a coyote?

3. Do you think Bill really invented the lasso and wrote cowboy songs? Explain.
4. Why do you think Bill's horse was named Widow Maker?
5. Why do you think Sue rode Bill's horse, even after Bill told her not to?
6. Write down a sentence from the story that you like. Explain why you like it.
7. Name one value that is respected in this tale and one value that is disliked. Give an example of each from the story. Choose from the following values:

bad temper	cleverness
wisdom	disobedience
motherhood	trust

Literary Element

Hyperbole

A *hyperbole* (hi-PER-bo-lee) is a figure of speech that uses great exaggeration. Hyperboles are often used to emphasize a point. They can be a good source of humor. Here is one example of a humorous hyperbole from "Pecos Bill":

"Pecos Bill felt his heart go up to his head, down to his feet, and back home again."

- *Write three hyperboles from the story. (Look for statements or events that are exaggerated and can't really be true.)*

BEYOND

Game

On your own, make a list of five difficult words from the story. Then play Hangman with a small group. Each person takes a turn in giving the others a word from the story.

Research

Find the words of two or more cowboy songs, such as "Home on the Range," and "Git Along Little Doggies." What do you learn about cowboys from these songs?

Creative Project

Write a song about Pecos Bill. Tell about some of the events that happened to him. Write the words to a tune you already know, such as "Jingle Bells."

Writing Project

Write a new adventure for Pecos Bill. Work in small groups. Each person writes the title and the first sentence to a new story. Then each person passes his/her paper to the right. Write the next sentence to the story you now have. Keep passing and writing until your original paper is returned to you.